ELECTRONIC DISCOVERY AND DIGITAL EVIDENCE
IN A NUTSHELL

By

SHIRA A. SCHEINDLIN
United States District Judge
Southern District of New York

DANIEL J. CAPRA
Philip Reed Professor of Law
Fordham University School of Law

The Sedona Conference®

A Thomson Reuters business

Mat #40806818

Thomson Reuters created this publication to provide you with accurate and authoritative information concerning the subject matter covered. However, this publication was not necessarily prepared by persons licensed to practice law in a particular jurisdiction. Thomson Reuters does not render legal or other professional advice, and this publication is not a substitute for the advice of an attorney. If you require legal or other expert advice, you should seek the services of a competent attorney or other professional.

Nutshell Series, In a Nutshell and the Nutshell Logo are
trademarks registered in the U.S. Patent and Trademark Office.

© 2009 Thomson Reuters

610 Opperman Drive
St. Paul, MN 55123
1–800–313–9378

Printed in the United States of America

ISBN: 978–0–314–20448–6   7000423

PREFACE

This "nutshell" is intended for both law students and practitioners. Law students studying civil procedure and evidence will find this relatively short narrative a helpful addition to the course. Those students who are taking courses in trial practice and federal discovery practice will also find this book quite useful. Practitioners, too, will find this a handy guide to issues that arise daily with respect to both discovery practice and trial practice. Civil litigation is primarily about discovery practice. The information that parties obtain during discovery from each other or from third parties will affect whether a case is tried, settled, or resolved by motion. Today, the vast majority of records are created and maintained electronically. Thus, "paper" discovery is a thing of the past and "e-discovery" is the present and the future. The creation and storage of electronic records, and the almost incomprehensible volume of such records, create new challenges regarding preservation and production. The same is true of trial practice. Much of the evidence admitted at trial consists of electronically created records—including documents, e-mail, databases, and spreadsheets. As you will see, this short volume discusses leading cases in this critical and developing area of law.[1]

To set the stage, we begin with a chapter (I) on the explosion of electronic information and how it is stored and retrieved. We turn then to a chapter (II) on the preservation of electronic information, covering such questions as when the duty to preserve attaches and what records must be preserved. We move on to a chapter (III) covering the required meeting between counsel at the outset of litigation, when counsel must address issues surrounding the discovery of electronic information. The next chapter (IV) provides much-needed guidance on how to collect data in order to disclose it during the discovery process. Once the data is collected, the big question is in what form will it be produced (Chapter V)—native format, TIFF, PDF, with or without metadata, etc. If the parties fail to produce relevant information the court must consider the imposition of sanctions based on the spoliation—including non-production and delayed production—of evidence (Chapter VI). Many issues that arise during e-discovery present difficult ethical issues (Chapter VII), such as whether a receiving party may engage in mining for metadata. When producing the equivalent of millions of documents, attorneys must carefully safeguard the client's privileges and protections (Chapter VIII). This chapter includes a discussion of the newly-enacted Rule 502 of the Federal Rules of Evidence. Finally, we address many of

---

1. To make the text easier to read, we have generally avoided footnotes altogether and have provided citations in the text. We have not given page citations for each quotation from a case.

the Rules of Evidence as they relate to the authentication and admissibility of digital evidence (Chapter IX).[2]

There are three co-authors of this Nutshell. Judge Shira A. Scheindlin was a member of the Advisory Committee on Civil Rules and a member of the Discovery Subcommittee that drafted the 2006 amendments addressing the discovery of electronically stored information. She is also the author of the landmark *Zubulake* opinions. Professor Daniel Capra of Fordham University School of Law is the Reporter to the Advisory Committee on Evidence Rules and the principal draftsman of Rule 502 on waiver of privilege. Finally, The Sedona Conference® has been the leading voice of the legal profession in addressing all of the concerns surrounding electronic discovery. Sedona has issued the most frequently cited publications in this area including the "The Sedona Principles: Best Practices Recommendations & Principles for Addressing Electronic Document Production" and "The Sedona Conference® Guidelines for Managing Information and Records in the Electronic Age." We wish to give special thanks to Kenneth J. Withers, Sedona's Director of Judicial Education and Content, who is one of the most knowledgeable people in the world on the topic of e-discovery.

We hope that the students and practitioners who use this Nutshell will find it useful, versatile,

2. For a fuller treatment of these issues, see Scheindlin, Capra, and The Sedona Conference®, *ELECTRONIC DISCOVERY AND DIGITAL EVIDENCE: CASES AND MATERIALS* (2008).

and well organized. It has been our privilege and pleasure to create this short volume, which addresses both the discovery and admissibility of digital records. We are convinced that absent knowledge of these cutting-edge issues, an attorney is simply not prepared to litigate in the twenty-first century.

SHIRA A. SCHEINDLIN
NEW YORK, N.Y.
DANIEL J. CAPRA
NEW YORK, N.Y.
THE SEDONA CONFERENCE®
PHOENIX, ARIZONA

April 2009

OUTLINE

Page

*

TABLE OF CASES

References are to Pages

XXI

TABLE OF CASES

TABLE OF CASES

TABLE OF STATUTES

UNITED STATES

UNITED STATES CODE ANNOTATED
15 U.S.C.A.—Commerce and Trade

FEDERAL RULES OF CIVIL PROCEDURE

TABLE OF STATUTES

FEDERAL RULES OF CIVIL PROCEDURE

TABLE OF STATUTES

FEDERAL RULES OF CIVIL PROCEDURE

TABLE OF STATUTES

FEDERAL RULES OF CIVIL PROCEDURE

FEDERAL RULES OF EVIDENCE

TABLE OF STATUTES

FEDERAL RULES OF EVIDENCE

RESTATEMENT 3RD FOREIGN RELATIONS LAW

ELECTRONIC DISCOVERY AND DIGITAL EVIDENCE
IN A NUTSHELL

*

CHAPTER I

THE EFFECT OF ELECTRONIC INFORMATION ON DIS- COVERY PRACTICE

A. EXPLOSION OF INFORMATION AND INCREASED SOURCES OF INFORMATION

"Modern instruments of discovery serve a useful purpose...." They together with pretrial procedures make a trial less a game of blindman's buff and more a fair contest with the basic issues and facts disclosed to the fullest practicable extent." *United States v. Procter & Gamble Co.,* 356 U.S. 677, 682 (1958) (internal citations omitted.) The way lawyers propounded and responded to discovery requests did not materially change between the 1930s and the 1990s, until the advent of office automation and the growth of the Internet. Document requests were made with the expectation that the receiving party, at counsel's direction, would devote sufficient resources to perform a reasonably diligent search for records found in hard-copy repositories including central file room areas and among work papers stored in offices. A recent article notes that:

Today, virtually all information is in electronic form. Electronically stored information grew at the rate of 30 percent annually from 1999 through 2002. ... The sheer volume is astounding. A data processing center for a major corporation can contain 10,000 tapes or more. One tape can store as much as 1 trillion bytes (1 terabyte) of information or even more. If converted to hard copies, information contained on a single tape would be the equivalent of a 200–mile–high stack of paper. The types of "discoverable" data in electronic form are also proliferating. Many are similar to previous hard-copy documents such as might be found in the printed output of Microsoft Word files and Excel spreadsheets. But discovery also includes more transitory forms that were never found in the pre-electronic world, with the primary example being e-mail messages.[1]

The conventional methods of conducting discovery, developed for a world of paper-based communication and record-keeping, are inadequate, costly, and occasionally irrelevant in a digital information environment characterized by volume and complexity. Well before the 2006 amendments to the Federal Rules of Civil Procedure established the distinct category of Electronically Stored Information ("ESI") with its own discovery rules, there was

1. James N. Dertouzos, et al., *The Legal and Economic Implications of Electronic Discovery: Options for Future Research*, RAND Institute for Civil Justice 1 (2008), *available at* http://www.rand.org/pubs/occasional_papers/ OP183.

widespread recognition that the volume and complexity of ESI presented different challenges for the practitioner.

The growth of digital information has continued to increase. The types and quantities of digital information an organization is likely to have today can be staggering. In the three year period from 2004 to 2007, the average amount of data in a Fortune 1000 corporation grew from 190 terabytes to one thousand terabytes (one petabyte). Over the same time period, the average data sets at 9,000 American, midsize companies grew from two terabytes to 100 terabytes. Overall, the global data set grew from five exabytes (five billion gigabytes) in 2003 to 161 exabytes in 2006. It is estimated that in 2007 the amount of information created and replicated globally surpassed 255 exabytes. A recent article commented on the litigation costs of coping with such a vast amount of data.

Take then, for example, litigation in which the universe subject to search stands at one billion e-mail records, at least 25% of which have one or more attachments of varying length (1 to 300 pages). Generously assume further that a model "reviewer" (junior lawyer, legal assistant, or contract professional) is able to review an average of fifty e-mails, including attachments, per hour. Without employing *any* automated computer process to generate potentially responsive documents, the review effort for this litigation would take 100 people, working ten hours a day, seven days a week, fifty-two weeks a year, over fifty-four *years* to complete. And the cost of such a review, at an assumed average billing of $100/hour, would be $2 billion. Even, however, if present-day search methods (such as in the tobacco litigation example) are used to initially reduce the e-mail universe to 1% of its size (i.e., 10 million documents out of 1 billion), the case would still cost $20 million for a first pass review conducted by 100 people over 28 weeks, without accounting for any additional privilege review.[2]

Given the amount of ESI that exists within the average organization, the ability to quickly and efficiently identify, locate, retrieve, and preserve the targeted set of ESI most likely to be responsive to the matter at hand becomes essential. In *Alexander v. Federal Bureau of Investigation,* 541 F. Supp. 2d 274 (D.D.C. 2008), also known as the "Filegate" case, plaintiffs filed a claim under the Privacy Act alleging that White House officials in the Clinton Administration violated the privacy rights of individuals by continuing to possess and access certain FBI files containing highly sensitive reports of interviews taken in connection with those individuals being nominated to positions requiring security clearances. Originally filed in 1996, the case bogged down in evidentiary proceedings related to the alleged loss of White House e-mail due to technical defects in the operation of the White House e-mail archiving system. A White House technician sub-

2. George L. Paul & Jason R. Baron, *Information Inflation: Can the Legal System Adapt?*, 13 Rich. J.L. & Tech. 10 (2007).

mitted a declaration stating that "all" e-mail had
been preserved on the "ARMS" system (Automated
Records Management System). Plaintiffs alleged
that this technician knew or should have known
that glitches had occurred resulting in the failure of
the ARMS system to capture a significant portion of
e-mail. Two million e-mails were eventually restored from backup tapes as a result of the lawsuit.
After holding over fifty days of hearings on the
subject of missing White House e-mail, the judge
eventually concluded that there had been misunder-
standings on the part of high level officials and
counsel, but no deliberate misconduct or wrongdoing in the filing of declarations or in making representations to the court.

> The Court has concluded that the essential
> errors made by the White House Counsel's Of-
> fice were caused by a lack of familiarity with
> computer terminology and language and work-
> ings by the lawyers involved. Mr. Barry, the
> computer expert, simply talked a different lan-
> guage, and the lawyers he dealt with did not
> fully appreciate the significance of some of the
> information that he gave them, and the infor-
> mation he didn't give them. All of this occurred
> long before development of current sophisticat-
> ed ways that lawyers have had to learn to deal
> with computer experts. It calls to the Court's
> mind its own experience in dealing with intelli-
> gence officials, *i.e.*, if you don't use the right
> words in your question, you won't get the right
> answer. You have to learn to ask the question

in a number of ways, and probe and examine and get into the nitty-gritty to understand what the truth is. None of the White House lawyers involved in this matter did that.

Writing in 2008 about events of many years earlier, the court noted that "[a]ll of this occurred long before development of current sophisticated ways that lawyers have had to learn to deal with computer experts."

B. HOW ELECTRONIC INFORMATION IS STORED AND RETRIEVED

Understanding what types of ESI are likely to play a role in e-discovery, the possible storage locations of such data, and the ways in which the targeted data may be organized have all become important factors in designing a focused and productive discovery effort.

1. Types of ESI

There are potentially thousands of different types of data that can exist within an enterprise data set. Typically, however, most organizations have a limited set of potential data types on a limited number of applications that create ESI. Thus, an important component of an ESI discovery plan is to identify the potential types of data that may yield responsive information. From the perspective of creating a discovery plan, there are two fundamental categories, or types, of ESI: (1) data created by individual custodians using local or enterprise applications; and (2) data created by individual custodians using an enterprise application and/or data which are automatically created or captured by an enterprise application.

a.   Custodian-Based ESI

Custodian-based ESI is familiar to anyone who uses a computer, as it is the data created by a person when using application programs on computers or through the use of personal digital devices such as cell phones and personal digital assistants ("PDAs").

b.   Application Data

An application is any program that is designed to perform a specific function directly for a custodian or, in some cases, for another application program. Examples of application programs include:

- Word processing programs
- Spreadsheet programs
- Database programs
- Web browsers
- Software development tools
- Graphical presentation programs
- Document publishing programs
- Sales and personal contact management programs

- Document scanning and storage programs
- Voice-to-text conversion programs
- Printed-text-to-digital-text conversion programs
- Draw, paint, and image editing programs
- Financial management programs
- Music management programs
- Text and other instant-messaging programs

c. Personal Digital Devices

A personal digital device is an electronic device operated by a custodian that is capable of creating ESI. Examples of common personal digital devices include:

- Cell phones
- PDAs
- Digital Cameras
- MP3 players, iPods, or similar device

d. Messaging Systems

Messaging systems are a special form of application in that they share characteristics of both custodian-based applications and enterprise applications. Most messaging systems are maintained in a central location and available for use by all those with an authorized account. The messaging system typically stores some custodian-specific messaging data at this central location. However, most messaging systems also allow the individual custodian to maintain some portion of her messaging data locally on her personal computer or at some other location she may designate. Examples of common messaging systems include:

- E-mail
- Electronic calendaring
- Voice mail
- Instant messaging

e.   Enterprise-Based ESI

Enterprise-based ESI is data that has been created by individual custodians using an enterprise-wide application, or which has been automatically created or captured by an enterprise-wide application, and is generally stored in a central location within the organization.

f.   Organization-Specific Applications

Organization-specific applications have been developed by teams of software developers that write special-purpose, company-specific application programs designed to automate part of the company's business function. For example, an agricultural products company may develop an application designed specifically for tracking its crops. These applications are typically enterprise in nature and are managed by the company's information technology ("IT") department.

g. Databases

Most organizations utilize database applications
to organize their finances, operations, inventory,
and business work flow. Databases often serve as
the content for other application programs, collecting and holding the information in a "structured"
fashion.

h. Generic Enterprise Applications

In addition to customized organization-specific
applications, many organizations employ standardized enterprise applications that have been designed
and built to solve a particular business need. Because these applications are generally available in
the marketplace, it is relatively easy to find information about the application and about the data
files that the application supports. Common examples of generic enterprise applications include:

i. Accounting

Automated accounting systems record and process the accounting transactions of an organization.
Most automated accounting systems are modular in
nature, allowing the organization to choose those
modules that it needs at the time, but also permitting it to add more functions when needed.

ii. CRM—Customer Relationship Management

CRM software is used to support customer contact systems and processes, typically by storing information on current and past customers, prospective customers, and sales leads. The information in the CRM application is available to employees in many departments including sales, marketing, product development, and customer service.

iii. EDRM—Electronic Document and Records Management

The purpose of an EDRM system is to enable an organization to manage its documents throughout the document life cycle, from creation to destruction. EDRM applications often associate a retention code with each record, thereby enabling the organization to destroy records once they have reached the end of their economic, regulatory, legal, or otherwise defined life cycle.

iv. ERP—Enterprise Resource Planning

An ERP system is an organizational support system based on a common database that integrates the data needed for a variety of business functions such as Manufacturing, Supply Chain Management, Accounting, Human Resources, and Customer Relationship Management.

v. PLM—Product Life Cycle Management

A PLM system provides an organization an automated platform to manage the entire life cycle of a product, from its conception, through design and manufacture, to service and disposal. It also provides the organization with a single source of all product-related information necessary for collaborating with business partners, for supporting product lines, and for developing new or enhanced product lines.

vi. SCM—Supply Chain Management

An SCM system provides an organization with an automated platform to plan, implement, and control all aspects of its supply chain by tracking the movement and storage of raw materials, work-in-process inventory, and finished goods from start to finish.

vii. SDLC—Systems Development Life Cycle

An SDLC system provides an organization an automated platform to manage the models and methodologies that the organization uses to develop systems, generally computer systems.

viii. SRM—Supplier Relationship Management

An SRM system provides an organization with an automated platform for managing its organizational buying processes, including the purchase of in-house supplies, raw materials for manufacturing, and goods for inventory.

i. Web-based Interfaces

Organizations use a variety of web-based interfaces to present unique applications and data and also to provide access to existing enterprise applications and data. Web-based interfaces are generally broken down into three categories:

i. Internet

The information presented on an organization's web site, and the information gathered from visitors to that web site, comprise a potentially vast source of ESI subject to discovery. Increasingly, organizations are connecting their Internet access points to databases and other application systems in an attempt to provide a low cost, single point of access to customers and prospective customers.

ii. Intranet

An intranet is a private computer network established by an organization that uses Internet protocols and network connectivity to create a private, in-house version of the Internet. Utilizing a familiar web browser interface, employees can access employee manuals, corporate calendars, updates on corporate events and milestones, records management policies, employee blogs, sales and marketing materials, stock quotations, and the like. Increasingly, intranets are being tied into corporate applications and databases in an attempt to provide a single-source interface to the company.

iii.   Extranet

An extranet is a private network established by an organization that uses Internet protocols, and network connectivity to create a private, in-house version of the Internet that is then shared with selected extra-organizational parties, such as vendors, suppliers, clients, and business partners. Utilizing a familiar web browser interface, those granted access to the organization's extranet can gain access to sales materials, catalogs, production updates, account information, e-mail, instant messaging, and blogs. Increasingly, extranets are being used to create virtual business communities where business partners come together to share information.

2.   How ESI Is Stored—Online, Near-Line, and Offline
a.   Online Storage of ESI

The definition of online as established by the United States General Services Administration calls for an online system to be available for immediate use on demand without human intervention, in operation, functional and ready for service. When ESI is stored online, the information is available to a user, on a computer system, in close to real-time.

Online storage devices are primarily hard drives, whether singly in a personal computer or connected together in an array in a networked system. From a discovery perspective, online data is relatively easy to identify, locate, search, retrieve and preserve.

b.   Near-Line Storage of ESI

Near-line storage is the storage of data on direct access removable media. When a near-line storage device is reattached to a computer system, the ESI stored thereon becomes available to the user online. The major categories of near-line storage include:

- Magnetic disks
- Compact disks ("CDs"), such as Recordable CDs ("CD–Rs"), Rewriteable CDs ("CD–RWs"), and Rewriteable Digital Versatile Disks ("DVD–RWs")
- Solid state storage (flash memory data storage device), such as memory cards and memory sticks (*e.g.*, USB flash drives)
- Removeable Direct Access Storage Devices ("DASDs") such as iPods and portable hard drives

Other devices that can serve as near-line storage devices include:

- Remote online backups
- Disk-based backups
- Printers, scanner, fax or photocopy machines with storage capability

While retrieval of ESI from a given near-line source is rarely an issue, retrieval from numerous near-line sources can create logistical and cost issues associated with the requirement for reintegrating the near-line storage device with the computer system before information can be retrieved.

c.   Offline Storage of ESI

Offline storage maintains ESI on a medium or a device that is not under the control of a processing unit and which is not available for immediate use on demand by the system without human intervention. The primary form of offline storage is magnetic tape. When used as a backup medium, online ESI is written to (stored on) a magnetic tape. The time and cost associated with restoring ESI from a magnetic tape is substantial compared with the cost of online or near-line access, and backup tapes are therefore used as a last resort. They must be retrieved, mounted and restored to the online system before any of the ESI on those tapes can be accessed. Given that backup tapes are used for backup, however, magnetic tape may be the only location on which particular data exists if it has been removed from all other online and near-line sources.

3. How ESI Is Stored from a Custodian/Records Management Point of View

From a technology standpoint, ESI can be stored on a variety of magnetic, optical, and solid-state media. The manner in which ESI is stored by the custodian or user onto these media can vary greatly, however, and has to do with both the organization's records management plan and the custodian's own desires regarding the naming and storage location of his or her data. There are five typical ways in which ESI can be stored:

a. Custodian-Centric Data Storage

Much of the ESI used by a custodian on a day to day basis is under the direct control of the custodian. It is the custodian who creates the content associated with a given data file, names it, and determines where the file will be saved. The custodian is also the default "records manager" for her data in the sense that she determines how long data will survive before being deleted. In terms of discovery, the custodian is often the best source of information about her data set, including:

- Types of data created (*i.e.*, what applications were used, including enterprise applications)
- Quantities of data created
- File naming conventions used
- Data storage locations
- Whether custodian-based backups were created

- Others with whom the custodian corresponded and/or shared files

- Use of e-mail and attachments

b. Virtual Workgroup-Centric Data Storage

A virtual workgroup is a group of individuals who work on a common project using digital technologies such as e-mail, instant messaging, shared application programs and databases, calendaring, and file management. While the custodian creates some of the content for the application data file, she may have little or no say in how the data file is named, where it is stored, how it is ultimately used, or how long it remains in existence. Many times these issues are handled either by organization rules or by a custodian named as the workgroup leader.

c. Business Unit-Centric Data Storage

Many organizations are structured like holding companies, made up of many business units that maintain their own computer operations but that share some overall application platforms, such as e-mail. A single organization may also have different operating divisions that it treats as business units. From the custodians' viewpoint, they are working on a single system. Behind the scenes, however, many different operating and data storage environments may be involved.

d. Enterprise-Centric Data Storage

Virtually every organization utilizes enterprise applications in its business model. One of the key characteristics of an enterprise application is that the data file(s) associated with the application are stored and managed at a central location within the organization, typically by professional computer services staff. E-mail is a common example of an enterprise application, but is distinguished by the fact that many e-mail systems allow users to maintain their incoming and outgoing messages both on the enterprise e-mail server and locally on their hard drives.

e. Third Party-Centric Data Storage

With the increased use of outsourced computer operations and the use of Internet-based applications, more and more organizational data are being stored and managed by third parties under a variety of contractual and logistical arrangements. Typically a user goes to a third party Internet site and logs onto an application program provided by the third party. The user then uses the application as if it resided on her desktop or on the enterprise computers. The data created by the user remains with the third party provider.

4. How Organizations Manage Backup ESI

a. Backups

Organizations typically make backups for three reasons. *First*, a backup protects the organization from losing its valuable data in case of a disaster (natural or manmade) or in case of a computer system failure that results in data loss. *Second*, a backup can be used to restore specific data files that have been accidentally deleted, modified, or corrupted. *Third*, many organizations use backups as a generic form of long-term data archiving. In this capacity, backups are made and are held by the organization as a central repository of data over time.

Backups are seldom the primary source of relevant ESI in discovery, and depending on the cost and burden of retrieval, backup ESI may be considered "not reasonably accessible" under Rule 26(b)(2)(B) of the Federal Rules of Civil Procedure and presumptively outside the scope of discovery. However, in litigation involving historical data that no longer exists in the active sources of ESI, a requesting party may be able to show "good cause" for discovery of ESI from backup sources. And Rule 26(b)(2)(B) does not absolve a party from the common law duty to take reasonable steps to identify and preserve sources of potentially relevant ESI for the duration of the litigation, including backup sources, even if they are not specifically requested in discovery. Therefore a thorough understanding of the client's backup ESI is necessary.

b.   Typical Categories of Backups

While a backup is technically any process that moves a file from its online storage location to another online, near-line or offline storage location, there are some typical ways in which backups are created by custodians and within organizations.

i.   Unstructured Backups

An unstructured backup is typically an ad-hoc copying of a small number of custodian-selected files to some form of online, near-line, or offline repository. Unstructured backups often have little or no information about what was backed up or when the backup took place, and there is little consistency to the frequency and/or content of such backups. Unstructured backups are probably the easiest to implement by the custodian, but they are the least managed and are prone to dispersal and loss.

ii.   Structured Backups

A structured backup is the backup of a predictable target set of data occurring on a set timetable. Structured backups, and especially those conducted systematically by an organization's computer services department, generally have detailed descriptions about what was backed up, when it was backed up, and how it was backed up.

iii. Local Backup

Local backups are conducted by custodians through the use of devices contained within, or attached directly to, their personal computer workstation. From a discovery perspective, local backups are usually sporadic in nature, stored in various locations, inconsistent in terms of types and quantities of data stored, and difficult to restore.

iv. Internet Backup

As high-speed Internet service has become more widely available and more robust, backup methodologies utilizing the Internet to create remote backup stores are growing in popularity. As remote Internet backup sites are generally organizationally and geographically removed, backing up data to the Internet can provide protection against geographically clustered disasters that could affect backup data stored in the same region as the host data.

v. Enterprise Backup

An enterprise backup is conducted by an organization's computer services staff involving business unit-level or organization-wide computer systems. A backup of an organization's e-mail system on a daily basis is an example of an enterprise backup. Because they are conducted by the organization's computer services staff for the purpose of providing a disaster recovery copy of the organization's data, enterprise backups tend to be the most structured in terms of the scope of the data targeted, the frequency of the backup, the consistency of the media onto which the backup is made, the recoverability of the backed up data, and the length of time the backup is maintained.

c.   Types of Backup Schemes

Within categories of backups there are different backup schemes that can be employed. Understanding the scheme chosen for a given backup is an important component in developing a proper model for restoring a backed up set of data, especially when restoring multiple backups to obtain data from a targeted time period. Typical backup schemes include:

i.   Full Backup

A full backup is a backup of every file on the targeted computer system, whether or not that file has changed since the previous backup. A full backup provides the fastest restoration time when restoring the full data set.

Example: If you perform a full backup every day of the week and the system crashes on Friday, you would need to restore the full backup set from Thursday to restore the data.

ii.   Incremental Backup

An incremental backup is a backup of every file on the targeted computer system that has changed since the last backup took place, regardless of whether the last backup was a full backup or an incremental backup. Because an incremental backup only targets those files that have changed since the last backup, which is typically a fraction of the total data set, it is usually the fastest type of backup and the one that requires the least storage space on the backup media. However, incremental backups also require the longest time and the most tapes to restore. Incremental backups are usually performed in conjunction with periodic full backups.

Example: If you perform a full backup each Sunday and incremental backups every night and the system crashes on Friday, you would need to restore the full backup from Sunday along with the incremental backups from Monday, Tuesday, Wednesday, and Thursday to restore the data.

iii. Differential Backup

A differential backup is a backup of every file on the targeted computer system that has changed since the last full backup. While a differential backup is not as fast as an incremental backup, it is faster than a full backup as it does not copy every file. Correspondingly, a differential backup requires more storage space than an incremental backup, but less than a full backup. When used in combination with a full backup, differential backups can provide an effective and efficient backup process.

Example: If you perform a full backup each Sunday and differential backups every night and the system crashes on Friday, you would need to restore the full backup from Sunday and the differential backup from Thursday.

iv. Continuous Data Backup

A continuous backup is a real-time backup that immediately logs every change on the targeted computer system to a secondary system. This is often done by saving byte or block-level differences rather than file-level differences, which fully utilizes the real-time nature of the system. Effectively, pieces of files are saved as they are changed. If restoration is needed, the management system knows how to piece everything back together in proper form. With a continuing decrease in hard disk storage costs, continuous backup, sometimes referred to as mirroring, may become more popular.

Example: If the system crashes on Friday, you simply restore the files from backup.

d. Backup Rotation

A backup rotation scheme is the method chosen for managing backup sets when multiple media are used in the backup process. The rotation scheme determines how and when each magnetic tape is used in a backup and for how long it is retained once it has backup data stored on it. The most common backup rotation scheme is referred to as the Grandfather–Father–Son model, which defines three sets of backups—daily, weekly and monthly.

The daily (Son) backups are rotated on a daily basis with one set graduating to weekly (Father) status each week. The weekly backups are rotated on a weekly basis with one graduating to monthly (Grandfather) status each month. Many organizations add to this model by removing one or more monthly tapes to an annual or multi-year storage.

Another common rotation scheme is to use a rolling set of magnetic tapes over and over again. This incremental model defines a pool of backup media and, once the entire pool has been used, re-writes to the oldest set. For example, a daily backup using a set of ten tape set holds ten days worth of individual daily backups. When all of the tape sets are used, the oldest one is inserted and re-used.

Tape rotation schemes can get very complicated based upon the needs of the organization. In terms of discovery, it is important to determine what tape rotation model is used and how it is implemented, as well as to understand that with any rotation model there will be gaps in the tape sets due to human, machine, or tape failures.

5.   Fundamental Computer Forensic Issues

We have now discussed data collection based on the way custodians and organizations create and store their data in the ordinary course of business— from the creation and storage of e-mail messages by users on their desktop computers, to the complex rotation of backup tapes by the IT department. While this level of volume and complexity would be enough to distinguish electronic discovery from conventional, paper-based discovery, electronic information systems provide another, even more technologically sophisticated method of collecting relevant ESI—computer forensics.

However, forensic collection is not required in most civil litigation. It involves the employment of experts, which is costly. It implicates issues of relevance, burden, privacy, and privilege. While forensic collection and examination is warranted in appropriate situations, it is not routinely required.

The primary question when considering forensic collection is whether or not the facts surrounding the matter at hand suggest that a forensic examination is needed. Were unique, important data deleted? Is it likely that deleted data can be recovered? Is it important to show usage activity and usage patterns? Is it important to authenticate a particular file in order to show that the represented data and/or time of creation is accurate? Do you need to confirm that all of the text in a document is original or that a critical e-mail was really sent when it appears to have been?

Because imaging software is commonly available, and because the vast majority of training programs in the field of electronic discovery revolve around forensics, there is a growing tendency to want to "image everything." But unless an argument can be made that the matter at hand will benefit from a forensic collection and additional examination, there is no reason to do a forensic collection just because the technology exists to do it.

If the matter allows for non-forensic acquisition and analysis of ESI, then a data collection is what is required. A data collection, as opposed to a forensic collection, collects files at the file level, not at the disk level, basically by copying the desired information and processing it into a review system. Data collection is faster and cheaper than a forensic collection and is the type of collection that is warranted if forensic collection is not required.

a.   Forensic Disk Images

When used in conjunction with discovery, the term "forensics" relates to the use of specialized techniques for the recovery, authentication, and analysis of specific ESI. Forensic examinations are typically used when a matter involves issues that require the reconstruction of computer usage patterns; the examination of residual data left after deletion; technical analysis of computer usage patterns; and/or other testing of the data that may be destructive in nature. In order to conduct a forensic examination, the ESI, and the storage device on which the ESI resides, must be collected in a manner that requires specialized expertise.

The most common form of forensic collection is to make an image of the storage media on which the targeted ESI resides. This image, sometimes called a bit image, bit-stream image, or a cloned image, is an exact copy of the storage device—such as a hard drive, a CD, or any other disk format—including all areas that contain data and all areas that appear to be empty (but which may actually contain fragments of data). The image is a single file containing the complete contents and structure of the storage device. A disk image file is created by making a sector-by-sector copy of the source media, thereby completely copying the entire structure and contents of the storage media. This image can be used to recreate an exact copy of the storage device on which a forensic examination can be conducted. The forensic examination can then be conducted on the recreated drive in exactly the same way in which it could have been done on the original device. Because forensic examinations often involve destructive testing, and because they require the ability to replicate their findings, this ability to work on recreated drives is critical.

b.   Recovering Deleted Files

A computer's file system determines how the computer stores and manages files on its attached storage media. There are several file systems in use today, and all offer some form of file recovery once a file is deleted. Consider the File Allocation Table ("FAT") file system, one of the most commonly used file systems today, as an example. Every computer file is recorded in the FAT directory. A file's directory entry is much like a person's listing in a telephone book. It holds the file's name and its storage location on a piece of storage media, such as a hard drive, a CD, or a DVD. The directory entry tells the computer where to find the data file. When a file is deleted on a FAT file system, its directory entry in the FAT remains stored on the disk, although the file name is altered in a way that lets the system know that the storage space occupied by the (now deleted) file is again available for use by a new file or by an expanded version of an existing file. The majority of the deleted file's information, such as its name, time stamp, file length and location on the disk, remain unchanged in its directory entry in the FAT. The deleted file's content will remain on the storage media until it is overwritten by another file. The more file activity there is on a particular computer system, the more unlikely it is that a file can be recovered, as the likelihood that the storage areas where the file had resided will be overwritten is greater.

Specialized software utilities, some provided with, or built into, the operating system, allow for the recovery of a deleted file provided that a new file or data set has not overwritten the areas of the storage device holding the deleted file in question. At the simplest level, these tools allow the modified file name of the deleted file to be changed back into a name format that does not indicate a deleted file. The file then becomes a ''live'' file again, and available for use by an application program. In some cases a greater level of reconstruction is required to retrieve some or all of a deleted file. If the directory entry for the deleted file has been overwritten, or if some of the data storage areas for the deleted file have been overwritten, it will be more difficult to recover the file.

Some computer operating systems provide a layered approach to data deletion. Microsoft's Windows platform, for example, does not really delete a file when a deletion request is made. The file is placed in a "recycle bin" where it awaits final deletion. Until the file is removed from the recycle bin, it can be easily recovered as it had not really been deleted in a technical sense. When the file is "dumped" from the recycle bin for deletion, it can often still be recovered if the space has not been reutilized.

As with forensic collection, the key question in discovery regarding the recovery of deleted data is whether or not the facts surrounding the matter at hand suggest that data recovery is needed. Was unique, important data deleted? Is it likely that deleted data can be recovered? Was the file located on a system where file activity was such that recovery is likely? Is the matter at hand one where file deletion is suspected or traditionally part of the pattern of activity for such matters, such as in trade secret theft? If the matter is one where deleted data recovery may be important, then attempts should be made to identify and recover appropriate files. If not, then deleted data recovery is not warranted and is ultimately a waste of time and resources.

As with imaging, data recovery software is commonly available, and because many of the training programs in the field of electronic discovery revolve around forensics (which is often targeted towards data recovery), there is a bias to target deleted data. But unless an argument can be made that the matter at hand will benefit from the recovery of deleted data, there is no reason to attempt such recovery just because the technology exists to do it.

CHAPTER II

PRESERVATION OF ELECTRONIC INFORMATION

A. RECORDS-RETENTION POLICIES

A records-retention policy is a set of official guidelines or rules governing storage and destruction of documents or ESI. Such policies typically define different types of records, how these records are to be stored, and often provide schedules defining specific time periods for retention of certain records. Regulatory, legal, business, or technical requirements may influence the duration of retention periods.

As the Supreme Court noted in *Arthur Andersen LLP v. United States*, 544 U.S. 696 (2005), there is nothing wrong with having a policy that requires the destruction of documents—as long as this destruction does not occur at a time when a legal duty to preserve has already arisen with respect to the documents to be destroyed under the policy. This is consistent with prior case law, which to some degree is codified in Rule 37(e) of the Federal Rules of Civil Procedure, providing that certain sanctions will not apply under ordinary circumstances where information is routinely destroyed before a duty to preserve has arisen.

Moreover, there are significant legal benefits to actively managing records retention. Consistent adherence to records-retention policies enables an enterprise to explain why certain records are available for production in discovery and why others are not. The availability of the "safe harbor" of Rule 37(e) is predicated, *inter alia*, on the ability to show some "routine" in the retention and destruction of records. Avoiding the cost of searching and reviewing millions of e-mails that have outlived their business utility and were under no regulatory or legal retention requirement is another major benefit.

Dealing with records retention issues is becoming more complicated as the volume and variety of ESI expands. While advances and cost reductions in storage technologies have facilitated the retention of large volumes of ESI, the determination of which records must be retained and which can be destroyed once the duty to preserve attaches is a difficult task. Suspending a function of a retention policy, such as the purging of e-mail from servers or the recycling of backup media, in order to comply with preservation obligations, can present significant challenges for legal and IT personnel. Not surprisingly, the issue of when and how to suspend records-retention policies when a duty to preserve arises has been the focus of much recent case law.

The *Arthur Andersen* case demonstrates that destroying records pursuant to a retention policy after the duty to preserve attaches is a risky business.

For a records-retention policy to act as a shield against spoliation allegations, the policy must have been implemented consistently. Where exhortations to comply with a policy's destruction requirements occurs *after* the duty to preserve attaches, compliance with the policy not only fails as a shield, but provides the very basis for a spoliation claim.

Most of the case law examining the issue of whether records were destroyed pursuant to routine records-retention policies involve business defendants. Accordingly, it is easy to forget that plaintiffs also have a duty to suspend regular destruction under records-retention policies once they plan to file suit.

Since the 2006 Amendments, including Rule 37(e), courts have continued to punish failures to suspend routine document destruction pursuant to records-retention policies in the face of a duty to preserve. These cases do not fault the policies themselves—just the failure to suspend such policies when faced with the need to apply a litigation hold. Examination of these cases shows the variety of types of retention policies applied to ESI and demonstrates the fundamental truth that there is no one-size-fits-all records-retention policy; instead, these policies should be designed to meet the "business and technical" needs of the party in question, as the Advisory Committee Note to Rule 37(e) suggests.

B. THE DUTY TO PRESERVE

The obligation to preserve evidence arises when a party has notice that the evidence is relevant to litigation or when a party should have known that the evidence may be relevant to future litigation. Identifying the boundaries of the duty to preserve involves two related inquiries: *when* does the duty to preserve attach, and *what* evidence must be preserved. Once a party reasonably anticipates litigation, it must suspend its routine document retention/destruction policy and put in place a litigation hold to ensure the preservation of relevant documents. The question of *when* a party should reasonably anticipate litigation is discussed in Section D (Trigger Date) below. The scope of the duty to preserve is discussed in Section E (Accessible and Not Reasonably Accessible ESI) below.

C. IMPLEMENTING THE DUTY TO PRESERVE

In *Zubulake v. UBS Warburg LLC* (*"Zubulake V"*), 229 F.R.D. 422 (S.D.N.Y. 2004), the court addressed counsel's obligation to ensure that relevant information is preserved by giving clear instructions to the client to preserve such information, ensuring that the client heeds those instructions, and then monitoring the client's compliance with those instructions. The goals of such a notice are to ensure that all sources of relevant information are identified, that these sources are carefully preserved for future review, and that relevant non-privileged materials are eventually produced to the opposing party.

1. Counsel's Duty to Locate Relevant Information

In order to identify all relevant information, counsel must identify how the client creates and stores its records, which requires meeting with IT personnel and all of the key players in a litigation to determine the sources on which potentially relevant records are stored. Only then can counsel construct and monitor a litigation hold notice.

2. Counsel's Continuing Duty to Ensure Preservation

Because Rule 26(e) requires a party to supplement its discovery responses whenever it "learns that in some material respect the disclosure or response is incomplete or incorrect" counsel has a continuing duty to ensure that relevant information is preserved, reviewed, and eventually produced. How is this best accomplished? The first step is to issue a litigation hold that is periodically re-issued. Identifying the best means of communicating the hold is left to the discretion of the party and its counsel, although regular e-mail alerts are quite effective. The next step is for counsel to communicate directly with those employees who are most likely to have knowledge and information relevant to the issues in the case to ensure that those employees are aware of their duty to preserve information and are preserving that information in a useful manner. The final step is for counsel to be sure that all sources of relevant information are identified and preserved, particularly if there are unique sources of information rather than merely duplicate or redundant sources. Backup tapes raise especially difficult questions with respect to preservation because they typically, although not always, contain duplicate information. It is fair to assume that a party need not maintain *all* of its backup tapes even after the onset of litigation. However, a party and its counsel should identify and safeguard backup tapes that are likely to contain relevant information that is not available from any other source. Such tapes should be segregated for safekeeping until they can be reviewed.

3. Do Non-Parties Have an Obligation to Preserve?

What if a party knows a non-party holds relevant information but does not itself have direct or constructive control over that information? Does the party have any obligation to ensure its preservation? If so, how can the party fulfill that obligation? Some courts have held that the party's preservation obligation includes the duty to inform the opposing party of the relevant evidence held by the non-party and the risk of its possible destruction. But what ability do litigants have to ensure the non-party preserves the relevant evidence? Does the notice by a party to the non-party that the information is relevant to potential litigation create a duty for the non-party to preserve it? If non-parties independently determine that the ESI they hold will be relevant to pending or future litigation involving others, does that knowledge create a non-party duty to preserve?

Generally, the answer to both questions is "no." Preservation of evidence, particularly of ESI, can be costly. Thus, courts have recognized that the obligations of non-parties to preserve evidence are different than those imposed on the parties. Unless the duty arises from a contractual agreement to preserve information or other special relationship that may give rise to the duty, non-parties generally do not have an obligation to preserve relevant data even when they anticipate that there may be a litigation in which such data are needed.

Some jurisdictions, however, recognize a common law tort for either intentional or negligent non-party spoliation of evidence where the non-party had reason to know of the litigation. Even in jurisdictions where no common law duty to preserve by non-parties is recognized, courts may still impose the duty where the non-party has a contractual or other special relationship with the party seeking preservation. An example of a relationship that might lead to a non-party duty to preserve is that between an insurance company and a policy holder involved in litigation. Where no such relationship exists, courts in jurisdictions not recognizing a common law tort of non-party spoliation may instead place the onus of non-party preservation on the party seeking it.

Although the following case involves the preservation of physical evidence rather than of ESI, it nicely illustrates the point. In *MetLife Auto & Home v. Joe Basil Chevrolet, Inc.*, 1 N.Y.3d 478 (2004), the New York Court of Appeals refused to recognize a common law tort for spoliation against a non-party auto insurer who had custody of a vehicle involved in a claim by a homeowner against an auto manufacturer. Even though the auto insurer had agreed verbally to preserve the evidence, the court declined to find a non-party duty to preserve because there was no relationship between the home insurer and the auto insurer. The court noted that the home insurer could have purchased the vehicle from the auto insurer, paid for the costs of preservation, or filed suit and issued a subpoena duces tecum on the non-party auto insurer. Because MetLife sued for the auto insurer's failure to preserve the vehicle *before* the claim in the primary suit was filed, it could not have issued a production or preservation subpoena on the auto insurance company. Thus, parties informed of the existence of relevant evidence held by non-parties before they have the ability to issue non-party subpoenas should consider taking other steps to ensure it is preserved. Courts, however, will not intervene in pre-litigation preservation disputes.

4. Preservation Obligations and Non-Party Subpoenas

Under Rule 45, if a non-party is served with a subpoena seeking documents or other production after an action has been filed, does the subpoena create an independent duty not only to produce the information, but also to preserve relevant information? Rule 45 is silent on the effect of a subpoena on the non-party's preservation obligations. If a subpoena creates both a production *and* a preservation obligation, how long should the non-party be required to preserve information, and what information must it maintain? In one recent case, the court held that a subpoena issued to a non-party imposes a preservation obligation on all information relevant to the subpoena until the non-party produces the requested materials and any disputes related to the subpoena are resolved. In another recent case, the court ordered a non-party to preserve evidence until motions to quash a non-party subpoena were resolved. After a recipient has fully complied with a subpoena, most courts hold that any preservation obligation that arose with service of the subpoena terminates. Additionally, while Rule 45 allows parties to serve subpoenas on non-parties, it does not require non-parties to produce ESI if it is not reasonably accessible, unless the issuing party can show good cause.

What if parties are unable to serve document subpoenas on non-parties holding relevant ESI even *after* the case is filed? How might they ensure relevant evidence is not destroyed? Under the Private Securities Litigation Reform Act, discovery in private securities fraud actions is stayed until a motion to dismiss has been decided unless discovery is necessary to preserve evidence or prevent undue prejudice to a party. The Act provides that, during the stay, *parties* have the obligation to preserve evidence as though document requests had been issued. But non-parties holding relevant evidence have no such statutory obligation. What can be done to ensure that non-parties holding relevant ESI and other evidence preserve it until the stay is lifted? Courts may permit parties to issue "preservation subpoenas" on non-parties. Even where non-parties' document retention and destruction policies may result in imminent destruction of relevant ESI, a party still needs permission to issue the subpoena.

5. Privacy and Preservation

Despite the existence of preservation obligations, federal privacy laws may prevent preservation and production of relevant ESI held by parties and non-parties. For example, the Stored Communications and Transactional Records Act prohibits providers of electronic communications services from disclosing the content of stored customer communications to any person, except the federal government upon a court-issued warrant. The Act has no exceptions for civil actions. Many other federal laws also limit disclosure of private information, but allow entities holding such information to disclose it in response to court-approved discovery requests.[1] For further examples of statutes prohibiting disclosure see Chapter V, infra, at 203–06.

Can contractual obligations regarding the privacy of customers' personal information limit the preservation obligations of a party or non-party? Suppose a web site host promises not to collect or store personal information about its users. Can the host be sanctioned for failing to preserve such information after the preservation obligation arose or be ordered to preserve such information going forward? What if the privacy policy is viewed as an integral part of the service offered by the host? In *Columbia Pictures Industries v. Bunnell*, 2007 WL 2080419 (C.D. Cal. May 29, 2007), plaintiffs sought the IP addresses of a web site's users who they alleged violated copyright law when using the site's file sharing service to trade copyrighted materials. The web site's privacy policy prohibited the site operator from collecting personal user information that the user unknowingly provided (*i.e.* provided automatically by the user's computer). As a result, the web site host did not preserve server log data, including the users' IP addresses. While the court held that the web site host must preserve such data,

1. *See, e.g.*, 15 U.S.C. §§ 6801(a), 6802, 6802(e)(8) (requiring financial institutions to protect privacy of customers' personal information, but permitting disclosure to respond to judicial process); *id.* § 6502(b) (prohibiting operators of web sites and other online services from disclosing personal information collected from children without parental consent, but providing an exception for response to judicial process).

the court concluded that IP addresses did not constitute personal information, finding that the addresses identified computers, not users. Thus, the
court never reached the issue of whether a party's
privacy policy could trump its preservation obligations or vice versa.

6. Preservation Obligations Under Federal Law

An independent obligation to preserve information may arise from federal or state statutes and
regulations requiring that certain types of data
be preserved, regardless of whether an entity is,
or may become, a party to litigation. For example, the Sarbanes–Oxley Act of 2002, passed in
the wake of high profile corporate accounting
scandals, requires publicly traded companies to
retain all records (including electronic records),
relating to audits for five years after the audit.
The Securities and Exchange Act, and the SEC's
regulations implementing it, impose extensive record retention requirements on stock exchanges,
members of the exchanges and securities dealers.
The Fair Labor Standards Act and corresponding
regulations require employers to retain payroll,
collective bargaining agreements and other employment contract records for three years; business volume records (in the form in which they
were maintained in the ordinary course of business) for three years; and employment and earn-
ing records, such as time cards, for two years.
The Department of Health and Human Services

requires health care providers that participate in the Medicare program to retain certain medical records for five years.

Although a party may have an independent duty to retain records under federal or state law, a violation of that obligation may not necessarily result in spoliation sanctions. In *Sarmiento v. Montclair State University*, 513 F. Supp. 2d 72 (D.N.J. 2007), an unsuccessful job candidate filed an employment discrimination claim against the University and sought sanctions in the form of an adverse inference against defendant for its failure to retain the selection committee's notes that related to the hiring decision. Plaintiff alleged, *inter alia*, that sanctions were warranted because the University violated federal regulations that required universities and colleges to retain hiring and other records.

The court explained that "[a]lthough a regulation may supply the duty to preserve records, a party seeking to benefit from an inference of spoliation must still make out the other usual elements" of that claim. Those elements included a requirement that the litigation be reasonably foreseeable; in this case, the court held that it was not.

D. TRIGGER DATE

1. When Does the Duty to Preserve Arise?

The 2006 Advisory Committee Note to Rule 37 states that: "A preservation obligation may arise from many sources, including common law, statutes, regulations, or a court order in a case." In addition, courts have held that the duty to preserve arises when a party knows, or reasonably should know, that the evidence is relevant to pending or future litigation. The point at which a party had actual knowledge or notice of pending or future litigation is relatively simple to identify. By contrast, determining when a party reasonably should have anticipated litigation—that is, when a party had constructive knowledge of future litigation—is a far more difficult question. It is often a key disputed issue during court consideration of spoliation motions. Broadly put, a party should preserve evidence when the party is on notice of a potential litigation or investigation.

2. How Should Parties Identify When the Duty to Preserve Has Been Triggered?

The determination of when the duty to preserve has been triggered is inherently fact specific. The Sedona Conference has suggested that in general, "[t]he determination of whether litigation is reasonably anticipated should be based on good faith . . . a reasonable investigation and an evaluation of the relevant facts and circumstances." Where a court must evaluate whether a party's decision to preserve or not preserve evidence was reasonable, the court should ask whether the party's decision was reasonable and made in good faith given the facts available to the party at the time it made the decision.

Anticipated litigation must be something more than a mere possibility or general discontent. 'The future litigation must be probable, which has been held to mean more than a possibility. The duty is likely triggered when a party provides unequivocal notice of its intent to file a claim, even if it has not yet filed a formal complaint. In general, reasonable anticipation of litigation arises when an organization is either on notice of a *credible threat* that it will become involved in litigation or it anticipates initiating litigation. But what facts and circumstances might suggest a credible threat? And how credible must that threat be?

When parties indicate a preference for negotiation, even though litigation is a possible outcome, the duty to preserve may not yet be triggered. In *Hynix Semiconductor Inc. v. Rambus, Inc.*, 591 F.Supp.2d 1038 (N.D. Cal. 2006), plaintiff's duty to preserve was not triggered when it contemplated litigation against copyright infringers only if negotiations failed and where the litigation depended upon other contingencies. Litigation became probable only when plaintiff interviewed litigation counsel. For other courts, the possibility of litigation may be sufficient to trigger the duty. In *Zubulake v. UBS Warburg LLC,* 220 F.R.D. 212 (S.D.N.Y. 2003) (*"Zubulake IV"*), an employment discrimination case, the court found the duty triggered when nearly all employees associated with Zubulake recognized the possibility that she might sue.

a. Plaintiffs' Duty to Preserve

When considering plaintiffs' duty to preserve, courts may be more likely to find the duty triggered before litigation formally commences than for defendants because plaintiffs control the timing of litigation. In *Cyntegra, Inc. v. Idexx Laboratories, Inc.*, 2007 WL 5193736 (C.D. Cal. Sept. 21, 2007), Cyntegra, a competitor of Idexx Labs, alleged that Idexx engaged in anti-competitive tying agreements with its buyers that severely disadvantaged Cyntegra's ability to generate revenue and profits. In March 2006, after Cyntegra failed to pay its data-storage provider, the provider deleted Cyntegra's files—including information relevant to Idexx's defense. Three months later, Cyntegra filed its claim. The court asserted that because plaintiffs control when litigation begins, they "must necessarily anticipate litigation before the complaint is filed." Because Cyntegra's injury resulted from conduct occurring prior to the data's destruction, the court concluded that Cyntegra must have anticipated litigation by that date. Although Cyntegra attempted to negotiate with Idexx to mitigate or eliminate the tying arrangements prior to filing suit, the court found that "[p]laintiff should have known that negotiation breakdowns were a distinct possibility, and that legal recourse might be necessary to prevent bankruptcy."

Even when a plaintiff does not file a claim until long after the conduct giving rise to the event occurred, the court may find that the plaintiff reasonably anticipated litigation. In *Silvestri v. General Motors Corp.*, 271 F.3d 583 (4th Cir. 2001), plaintiff claimed his injuries sustained in a car accident were exacerbated when the vehicle's air bag failed to deploy. After the accident, Silvestri nearly immediately retained counsel, who in turn hired experts who inspected the vehicle and the accident site within weeks of the accident. One expert concluded that there was a valid case against GM because the air bag should have deployed. The experts asserted their understanding that the inspection was conducted in anticipation of litigation and suggested to plaintiff's counsel the need to preserve the vehicle for GM's inspection. A few months after the accident, the owner of the vehicle sold it and the new owner repaired the damage, preventing GM from inspecting the car in its damaged state. On these facts, the court found that Silvestri anticipated litigation shortly after the accident and the duty to preserve was triggered at that time.

b. Pre-Filing Communications Between Counsel

Pre-filing communications between the litigants or their counsel can also provide constructive notice that litigation is likely. Demand letters stating a claim may be sufficient to trigger an obligation to preserve depending on whether the clarity and content of pre-filing communications reasonably suggested litigation. While something less than a clear indication of intent to sue may be sufficient to trigger the duty, correspondence that merely presents a basis for the dispute may be inadequate. In *Cache La Poudre Feeds LLC v. Land O'Lakes, Inc.*, 244 F.R.D. 614 (D. Colo. 2007), the court held that defendant's duty to preserve evidence was *not* triggered by an "equivocal" pre-filing communication that did not threaten litigation, suggested initial interest in avoiding litigation, and did not demand preservation of relevant materials.

When a party receives pre-filing correspondence from opposing counsel that is suggestive of potential litigation, but neither specifies the nature of, or events giving rise to, the claim, nor explicitly threatens litigation, does the duty to preserve impose any obligation on the recipient to further investigate to determine whether a litigation threat exists? In *Stallings v. Bil-Jax, Inc.*, 243 F.R.D. 248 (E. D. Va. 2007), the court found that although a letter from plaintiff's counsel was vague, it "provided some notice to [defendant] that Stallings might bring a lawsuit against it ... [and defendant] had ample time to make a timely request for additional information regarding the nature of the incident referred to in the letter." Thus, the court found that defendant was at least partially responsible for the destruction of relevant evidence.

c. Pre-Filing Preservation Letters

While discovery requests clearly put a party on notice of the relevance of data requested, what

about pre-filing preservation letters? Although the
common law duty of preservation does not depend
on receipt of a preservation letter, the court in
Cache La Poudre stated that "prudent counsel
would be wise to ensure that a demand letter ...
addresses ... preservation obligations." Properly
crafted pre-litigation preservation letters can impose the duty of preservation. For example, in *Gar-
rett v. Albright*, 2008 WL 681766 (W.D. Mo. Mar. 6,
2008), the court held that a plaintiff's preservation
letter sent six days after a fatal accident seeking
preservation of the tractor-trailer allegedly at fault,
and another request eighteen days after the accident for preservation of driving records and on-
board electronic tracking devices were specific as to
evidence requested and put defendant on notice
that litigation was imminent.

Can broad or overly inclusive preservation letters
successfully trigger a pre-litigation duty to preserve
all the information requested? In *Frey v. Gainey
Transportation Services, Inc.*, 2006 WL 2443787
(N.D. Ga. Aug. 22, 2006), the court declined to
impose sanctions on defendant for failing to preserve evidence demanded by plaintiff in a pre-filing
letter sent fifteen days after the incident giving rise
to the claim and ten days before the claim was filed.
While the fact that plaintiff retained counsel should
have put defendant on notice that litigation was at
least a "possibility," the court noted that compliance with the fifteen-page demand letter would
have required defendant to preserve virtually all
business records and would have exceeded allowable

discovery under the Federal Rules of Civil Procedure.

If the preservation request is too narrow, does the receiving party have a duty to preserve relevant evidence not mentioned in the letter? In *Healthcare Advocates, Inc. v. Harding, Earley, Follmer & Frailey*, 497 F. Supp. 2d 627 (E.D. Pa. 2007), the court rejected plaintiff's assertion that defendant had notice of its duty to preserve temporary cached files containing web site screen shots when plaintiff's subpoena sought production of computers and *copies* of archived screen shots, requested that nothing be deleted or altered on the computers, and notified defendant that its accessing of archived copies of plaintiff's web pages may have violated federal law. The court noted that while defendant had preserved the copies, it had no duty to preserve the cached files because the letter had not requested preservation of temporary cached files. Moreover, the court noted that defendant could not have reasonably understood the letter to impose such a duty when defendant had never saved the cached files to the computers' hard drives.

d.   Closely Related Proceedings

Closely related investigations or proceedings involving similar facts and claims can also provide pre-filing constructive notice of future litigation. In *Zubulake*, the court identified the trigger date as the day on which plaintiff's discrimination complaint was first filed with the Equal Employment

Opportunity Commission ("EEOC"). An EEOC complaint at least provides the possibility of a civil suit and clearly puts an employer on notice that either a suit by the federal government or the complainant is likely to follow.

E. WHAT RECORDS MUST BE PRESERVED? ACCESSIBLE AND NOT REASONABLY ACCESSIBLE ESI

In *Zubulake IV*, the court discussed the scope of the duty to preserve ESI. The court began by noting that all relevant documents must be preserved and that a litigant should be free to choose how best to accomplish this task. The court provided examples of mirror-imaging of all hard drives, preservation of all backup tapes, and data collection from key players. None of these examples were meant to create ironclad rules of what must be done to preserve relevant ESI. Rather, they were meant to illustrate that once the duty to preserve arises a party must suspend its routine document retention/destruction policy and create a litigation hold to ensure the preservation of relevant documents.

This opinion was issued prior to the 2006 Amendments and was an early attempt to distinguish between accessible and inaccessible ESI. The court determined that backup tapes held solely for disaster recovery were inaccessible, whereas those accessed in the regular course of business were accessible. It also carved out an exception for backup tapes of key players, if data found on those tapes were not available from a more accessible source and were likely to contain relevant information.

1.   What ESI Must Be Preserved?

Zubulake IV makes clear that the duty to preserve applies to *all relevant* information, including ESI, in the possession, custody or control of a party regardless of where it is located. Given that ESI is involved in virtually every aspect of daily communications, a broad interpretation of that duty could require preservation of extensive amounts of data. One court defined the types of relevant data that may be covered by a preservation obligation:

"Documents, data, and tangible things" shall be interpreted broadly to include writings, records, files, correspondence, reports, memoranda, calendars, diaries, minutes, electronic messages, voice mail, E-mail, telephone message records or logs, computer and network activity logs, hard drives, backup data, removable computer storage media such as tapes, discs and cards, printouts, document image files, Web pages, databases, spreadsheets, software, books, ledgers, journals, orders, invoices, bills, vouchers, check statements, worksheets, summaries, compilations, computations, charts, diagrams, graphic presentations, drawings, films, charts, digital or chemical process photographs, video, phonographic, tape or digital recordings or transcripts thereof, drafts, jottings and notes, studies or drafts of studies or other similar

such material. Information that serves to identify, locate, or link such material, such as file
inventories, file folders, indices, and metadata,
is also included in this definition.[2]

But there are some limitations on the scope of the
duty to preserve: it does not include every shred of
paper, every e-mail or electronic document, and
every backup tape.

The degree to which ESI is accessible bears on
the preservation obligation. *Zubulake IV* held that
inaccessible ESI must be preserved only if it is
relevant to the litigation and is not available on a
more accessible source. Why are backup tapes used
only to restore a system considered to be not reasonably accessible? The answer is that backup tape
systems not designed for routine retrieval are not
readily usable. Such systems indiscriminately capture all information at a given time and from a
given server but typically do not catalogue the information by subject matter. Thus, ordinarily, parties need not suspend their routine systems for
overwriting tapes even when they are aware that
the duty to preserve has been triggered. However, if
a party knows, or should have known, that the ESI
contained on the tapes is potentially relevant to the
claim and that this information is non-duplicative of
other accessible information, that party must safeguard the tapes even if they are considered to be
inaccessible.

2. *In re Flash Memory Antitrust Litig.*, 2008 WL 1831668
(N.D. Cal. Apr. 22, 2008).

2. Is Mere Relevance Enough to Trigger the Duty to Preserve Not Reasonably Accessible ESI?

Under *Zubulake IV*, all *relevant* ESI, even if inaccessible, must be preserved regardless of cost, if the information is not available in another accessible form. The Federal Rules likewise suggest that the mere fact of inaccessibility does not relieve a party of its preservation obligation. Other courts have taken a contrary view, finding the duty to preserve does not cover inaccessible ESI regardless of its relevance to potential litigation.

If mere relevance triggers the duty to preserve inaccessible ESI, how do parties determine whether the information is relevant? Evaluating preservation obligations based on relevance poses particular difficulties for parties at the pre-litigation stage before parties have had the opportunity to meet and confer on preservation issues. How should parties assess *ex ante* the potential relevance of ESI before a claim has been filed? Pre-litigation assessment necessarily depends on what the party knew or should have known about the potential claim before it was filed.

Should there be a requirement for *heightened* relevance before parties are required to preserve inaccessible ESI? Must the ESI be particularly relevant to the litigation to justify costs and burdens of preserving inaccessible ESI? In *Best Buy Stores L.P. v. Developers Diversified Realty Corp.*, 247 F.R.D.

567 (D. Minn. 2007), defendants sought sanctions where plaintiff downgraded a once accessible database into an inaccessible format. The court rejected sanctions in the absence of a showing that the database was of "particular relevance to this litigation," noting that because of the breadth and nature of the information in the database, it would have been "relevant to virtually any litigation involving [plaintiff]."

3. Should the Costs of Preserving Not Reasonably Accessible ESI Bear on the Duty to Preserve It?

Should potential relevance be weighed against the costs of preserving inaccessible ESI? In *McPeek v. Ashcroft*, 202 F.R.D. 31 (D.D.C. 2001), the court relied upon the concept of the "marginal utility" of the ESI when considering production obligations for relevant but inaccessible information stored on backup tapes. Noting that it would be impossible to know in advance what information might be on the tapes, the court weighed the "theoretical possibility" that the backup tapes would contain information relevant to the claim against the high financial and human resource costs of restoring the tapes, but could not resolve the conflict without gathering more information. Nonetheless, the court was concerned that the time and cost involved in restoring tapes would detract from defendant's other responsibilities. In the end, the court required the Department of Justice to do a "test-run" and restore a limited number of tapes so that it could determine both the cost of restoration and the yield of relevant information.

4. Does Downgrading ESI From an Accessible to an Inaccessible Format Violate the Duty to Preserve?

If information is reasonably accessible when the duty to preserve is triggered, what obligations do parties have to maintain that information on accessible storage media? The court in *Best Buy Stores* recently considered this question. Plaintiff had developed a database for use in unrelated litigation that remained intact and searchable at the onset of discovery. However, Best Buy later transferred the original data—from which the database depended—to inaccessible backup tapes. The court held that plaintiff had no duty to maintain the data in an accessible form because, in part, preservation costs would have exceeded $27,000 per month.

A similar question was at issue in *Quinby v. WestLB AG*, 2005 WL 3453908 (S.D.N.Y. Dec. 15, 2005). There, the court declined to impose sanctions on a defendant that transferred relevant e-mails from an accessible to inaccessible format well after it had notice of potential litigation because it found the duty to preserve does not include "a duty to keep the data in an accessible format." In a later decision, however, the court required defendant to bear the recovery costs since it should have known the transferred ESI would be relevant to later litigation.

5.   Does the Duty to Preserve Include Metadata Embedded in ESI?

Metadata are information about a particular data set that describe how, when and by whom it was collected, created, accessed, modified and how it was formatted. Converting a file from its original, or "native," format—the form in which the file was created—into an image file, such as Adobe Portable Document Format ("PDF") or Tagged Image File Format ("TIFF"), strips the metadata, providing only a static image of the document. In addition, "stripping" technology exists to remove metadata without converting documents to other formats. Some ESI, such as databases and spreadsheets created using formulae and linked-data sources, cannot be stripped of metadata without losing substantial information.

Does the duty to preserve relevant ESI include preservation of documents in their native format? Metadata in the production context may provide valuable information. Rule 34 requires that documents be produced "as they are kept in the usual course of business" and, unless otherwise specified by the requesting party, in the "form ... in which [they are] ordinarily maintained or in a reasonably usable form." The 2006 Advisory Committee Note to Rule 34 illustrates the Rule's intent:

[T]he option to produce in a reasonably usable form does not mean that a responding party is free to convert [ESI] from the form in which it is ordinarily maintained to a different form that makes it more difficult or burdensome for the requesting party to use the information efficiently in the litigation. If the responding party ordinarily maintains the information it is producing in a way that makes it searchable by electronic means, the information should not be produced in a form that removes or significantly degrades this feature.

This commentary suggests that metadata may not be stripped if it makes the documents less useful or less searchable. The Commentary to the 2007 Revised Sedona Principles makes a different but related point: while ESI may have had certain metadata when it was created, that metadata may not have been maintained when the information was stored for ordinary business purposes.

Metadata can be valuable because it provides information directly relevant to the claim, may help authenticate a document, and may aid in document management. For example, metadata may be directly relevant to a copyright infringement claim because it can demonstrate who copied, accessed or modified a file. However, one court asserted that "[m]ost metadata is of limited evidentiary value, and reviewing it can waste litigation resources."[3]

3. *Wyeth v. Impax Labs., Inc.*, 248 F.R.D. 169 (D. Del. 2006) (citing *Williams v. Sprint/United Mgmt. Co.*, 230 F.R.D. 640 (D. Kan. 2005)).

What if the *only* value of the metadata is their ability to aid in document management during the litigation—that is, they provide no *substantive* information, but allow very large quantities of ESI to be easily grouped and searched? In this example, preserving and producing otherwise irrelevant metadata could be important in conserving litigation resources.

In *In re Payment Card Interchange Fee & Merchant Discount Antitrust Litigation*, 2007 WL 121426 (E.D.N.Y. Jan. 12, 2007), defendants objected to plaintiffs' production of relevant e-mails in TIFF format because it degraded their searchability, even though the TIFFs would be searchable if subject to optical character recognition. The court required plaintiffs to produce e-mails in their native format, finding that the TIFF conversion ran "afoul of the Advisory Committee's proviso that data ordinarily kept in electronically searchable form should not be produced in a form that removes or significantly degrades this feature." Given that metadata may have inherent value to searchability and document authenticity, there may be a rebuttable presumption that metadata are relevant even when the metadata provide no substantive information that directly relates to the claims or defenses.

Some courts have issued preservation orders that explicitly include metadata among the categories of ESI that parties must preserve, or have required preservation of electronic documents in their native format. In *Hagenbuch v. 3B6 Sistemi Elettronici Industriali S.R.L.*, 2006 WL 665005 (N.D. Ill. Mar.

8, 2006), the court rejected defendant's argument that TIFF documents provided all the relevant information plaintiff needed, holding that the metadata would "allow [plaintiff] to piece together the chronology of events and figure out, among other things, who received what information and when." For a further discussion of cases requiring the production of metadata, see Chapter V, *infra*.

F. DOES ESI INCLUDE EPHEMERAL DATA?[4]

Transitory or ephemeral data pose particular difficulties for parties considering the scope of their preservation obligation. Ephemeral data has been defined by Ken Withers of the Sedona Conference as "data not to be stored for any length of time beyond their operational use and ... susceptible to being overwritten at any point during the routine operation of the information system." Temporary cache files of web pages visited present the classic example of ephemeral data: users surf the web, web pages are temporarily cached on their computers to allow the web page to load quickly when it is next accessed, and then overwritten as the cache storage fills up. Many other forms of transitory data exist. The Sedona Principles suggest that courts should

4. For a thorough and thoughtful discussion of the need to preserve ephemeral data stored in random access memory ("RAM") see *Columbia Pictures Indus. v. Bunnell*, 2007 WL 2080419 (C.D. Cal. May 29, 2007), *aff'd*, 245 F.R.D. 443 (C.D. Cal. Aug. 24, 2007) (ordering preservation of server log data in copyright infringement case).

not require extraordinary efforts to preserve "particularly transitory" ESI.

To date courts have not sanctioned parties for failing to preserve ephemeral data. A key question for courts considering the issue may be whether ephemeral data are actually "stored" in any meaningful sense. In *Healthcare Advocates, Inc. v. Harding, Earley, Follmer & Frailey*, 497 F. Supp. 2d 627 (E.D. Pa. 2007), the court rejected sanctions on defendant law firm for failure to preserve temporary cache files of archived web pages accessed through a non-party, public web site. Defendant accessed the archived pages in an effort to gather evidence to defend its clients in an unrelated case brought by plaintiffs and preserved copies of the accessed pages relevant to that case. The court noted that the cached files were not apparently relevant to the pending claim, were deleted automatically, and may have "been lost the second another website was visited."

In *Convolve, Inc. v. Compaq Computer Corp.*, 223 F.R.D. 162 (S.D.N.Y. 2004), the court rejected sanctions for defendant's failure to preserve data on an electronic device used to "tune" computer hard drives, where the data collected from the device were automatically overwritten with subsequent measurements. The court noted that in contrast to e-mail, "the data at issue here [were] ephemeral" and defendants had no business reason to maintain them as "[t]hey exist[ed] only until the tuning engineer [made] the next adjustment, and then the document change[d]."

Ken Withers has suggested that courts should consider four factors in deciding whether ephemeral data should be preserved: (1) whether the data are uniquely relevant to the litigation; (2) how the data are ordinarily treated by the party "in the ordinary course of business;" (3) whether preservation imposes excessive costs or burdens relative to the value of the data; and (4) whether technologies exist to preserve the data. Just as ESI's accessibility may depend on evolving technologies that make formerly cost-prohibitive restoration economically viable, any obligation to preserve ephemeral data may depend, in part, on whether technologies exist to preserve them in a non-transitory state, and the costs associated with implementing those technologies.

G. LITIGATION HOLDS/MONITORING

Cache La Poudre, cited earlier in this Chapter, provides a very interesting discussion of a litigant's duty to institute and monitor a litigation hold. Within days of being sued defendant initiated a litigation hold. The company searched for electronic documents in the possession of current employees, and created printed versions of electronic documents generated by employees who had left the company. No one tried to find electronic versions of documents created by former employees based on the attorneys' belief that those materials no longer existed because the IT department routinely cleaned an employee's computer hard drive when they left the company.

Each current employee involved in the subject matter of the suit was asked to find responsive materials and deliver them to counsel to be reviewed for relevancy. Counsel confirmed that the employees understood their task, and also reconfirmed that employees had produced all the required materials. But counsel admitted that he relied on the employees' ability and discretion in locating and delivering responsive documents. Defendant conceded that it never reviewed any backup tapes and that it made no effort to contact former employees. As a result, plaintiff argued that defendant failed to properly discharge its obligation to locate, preserve and produce all relevant, non-privileged materials and to properly monitor compliance with its discovery obligations. The court found one important violation of defendant's discovery obligation: continuing to clean the hard drives of former employees eliminated a readily accessible source of potentially relevant information. The court noted that "once a 'litigation hold' has been established, a party cannot continue a routine procedure that effectively ensures that potentially relevant and readily available information is no longer 'reasonably accessible' under Rule 26(b)(2)(B)."

In general terms, the court noted that a "litigation hold" is only the first step in the discovery process. A party must still conduct a reasonable search for responsive documents. Without more, a litigation hold will not satisfy the "reasonable inquiry" requirement of Rule 26(g)(2). The court stated that "counsel retains an on-going responsibility to take appropriate measures to ensure that the client has provided all available information and documents which are responsive to discovery requests." The court ultimately found that although defendant's actions had not substantially prejudiced plaintiff, its failure to halt the wiping of former employees' hard drives and to adequately monitor the litigation hold "interfered with the judicial process" and "forced Plaintiff to incur additional litigation expenses." As a result, the court imposed a small monetary sanction on defendant.

1. What Should an Organization Do After the Duty to Preserve Arises?

After an event triggers the duty to preserve, company officials, in-house lawyers and outside counsel should quickly meet to determine the claims, defenses, and key issues in a case. Once identified, the claims and defenses are assessed with respect to each element that will be at issue if the claim is litigated. The assessment team must then determine where relevant information resides, typically by first identifying those employees who generate, receive or otherwise access potentially relevant information. Each employee will have numerous potential data locations that must be preserved. At this point representatives of the company's IT and Records Management Departments must join the team. Armed with knowledge of the issues and the employees who are likely to have relevant information, counsel, company management, records manager, and IT representatives can begin to locate and secure relevant ESI. Referring to the company's document retention policy will also assist the team in determining where certain kinds of information are located, or whether those sources of information are no longer available.

2. How to Preserve Relevant Data?

Counsel must issue a litigation hold notice once a duty to preserve has been determined. This notice is addressed to those persons within the company who are custodians of data locations where relevant data might lie. Here is an example of a litigation hold notice in a hypothetical case involving the alleged failure to consummate the purchase of goods.

LITIGATION HOLD NOTICE
DIRECTIVE TO CEASE DESTRUCTION OF PAPER RECORDS AND ELECTRONIC DATA

TO: Distribution List

FROM: General Counsel

DATE:

Defendants have recently been sued in a dispute involving purchase orders and products sold by Plaintiff. We intend to vigorously defend this lawsuit.

The law requires us to take immediate steps to preserve all **paper records** and **electronic**

data that are relevant to the litigation. Paper records and electronic data (**including duplicates**) must be preserved at all storage locations including your office computer, home computers, and other portable electronic media such as discs and thumb drives. Failure to preserve all paper records and electronic data may result in legal sanctions.

Please immediately review the following list of **preservation categories** of documents (paper and electronic data) which must be preserved. All electronic data and paper documents including drafts, e-mail negotiations and communications related to or about any of these categories must be preserved.

1. All documents related to any contract, negotiation, or communication with Plaintiff.

2. All documents related to contracts and agreements with Plaintiff, including guarantees.

3. All paper rebates submitted and processed by Defendants related to consumer purchases of Plaintiff's products. All rebate processing data and information stored in any database pertaining to Plaintiff's products.

4. All financial and accounting records pertaining to Plaintiff.

5. All notes, memoranda, and spreadsheets related to Plaintiff.

6. All advertisements and promotions of Plaintiff's products.

7. All documents and data about customer service pertaining to Plaintiff's products.

8. All documents and data regarding the receipt of Plaintiff's products.

9. All shipping and receiving documents and data regarding Plaintiff's products.

10. All returns of Plaintiff's products and all consumer complaints about Plaintiff's products or the quality of Plaintiff's products.

11. All information about the flat screen television market and market pricing of flat screen televisions during 2006 and 2007.

12. All consumer inquiries and complaints about Plaintiff-related rebates.

13. All documents and data about any audit or accounting with respect to Plaintiff rebates.

14. All documents and data about the advertising and promotion of Plaintiff's products.

Please determine immediately whether you have in your possession, custody or control **any paper or electronic data about, concerning, or related to** any of the above preservation categories. Such paper documents or electronic data are called responsive paper documents or electronic data.

Please determine whether any responsive data is located on your laptop or office computer, home computer, Blackberry, PDA, discs, CDs, DVD's, memory sticks, or thumb drives, or any other electronic storage location. Please immediately suspend the deletion (manual or automatic) of relevant electronic data from any location where you believe responsive data may be found.

With respect to paper documents, please check all your office files and home files. Please immediately suspend the destruction of any responsive paper documents.

If you have any doubts about what paper or electronic data to preserve, please contact me. If you have any responsive paper documents please immediately advise your supervisor. If you have any responsive electronic data held or stored at any location or on any media **other than your office desktop computer or company laptop**, please immediately advise your supervisor.

———————

Once counsel has issued the litigation hold notice, her work is not over as counsel has a continuing duty to ensure that discoverable information is not lost. Thus, the following additional steps should be considered:

- suspending the routine document retention/destruction policy;

- becoming fully aware of the client's document retention policies and data retention architecture;

- communicating with the key players in the litigation to understand how they stored information;

- taking reasonable steps to monitor compliance with the litigation hold so that all sources of discoverable information are identified and searched; and

- having identified all sources of potentially relevant information, retaining that information and producing information responsive to the opposing party's requests.

Compliance with a litigation hold is not a simple matter. The purpose of the litigation hold is to notify the recipients of the obligation to preserve data. To ensure the litigation hold is followed and implemented, counsel should require a signed certification by the employee that the litigation hold notice has been received, understood and implemented. Here is an example of such a certification or acknowledgment.

Acknowledgment

(Please provide to your immediate supervisor)

I acknowledge I have read the above attached Litigation Hold memorandum. I will immediately conduct a reasonable search for responsive paper documents and electronic data. I will preserve any such electronic data and paper documents. I will not delete any data from any locations that I believe may contain responsive electronic data. I understand that this preservation request is ongoing and requires the continuing preservation of data, including data created or received both before and after receipt of this Notice.

_____

(sign and date)

_____

Other problems associated with compliance and implementation of a litigation hold arise when there is negligence or malfeasance. For example, would it be foreseeable that an employee who has received a litigation hold notice instructing her not to destroy any ESI associated with a particular company deletes e-mail in one folder because she knows the e-mail is retained in a second folder in her inbox or because she understands that the sender of the e-mail has created a special folder that contains the e-mail? The notion that duplicative e-mails and near duplicates of e-mail must be retained is something counsel may grasp but is easily misunderstood by employees. What if the employee prints all the relevant e-mails and then deletes the electronic files? The employee might reasonably think all e-mail has been retained, when, in fact, the deletion constitutes spoliation.

With these concerns in mind, after the delivery and receipt of confirmation of the litigation hold notice, counsel should schedule an interview with each custodian to review the custodian's data and how they must be preserved. Even if the company's IT representative has already given counsel a detailed description of what sources of company data an employee may use that are relevant to the litigation, the IT representative may have no way of knowing that a particular custodian also maintains company data relevant to the case on a personal computer at home or a portable personal USB drive. With the advent of free and unlimited e-mail storage on internet service providers like Yahoo or AOL, employees may frequently send work e-mails to their personal accounts to get around storage limits imposed on their corporate e-mail accounts. Document collection interviews with key custodians also give counsel the opportunity to confirm that the custodian has understood what is expected, and more importantly, that counsel knows the custodian has attempted to comply with the litigation hold.

3. Lifting Litigation Holds

Much time and money is spent on properly implementing and maintaining a legal hold, but little attention is given to lifting a legal hold. A legal hold may be lifted once the litigation is finally resolved, assuming that preserved data are not relevant to any other existing or anticipated litigation. This can be a difficult challenge if a company is simultaneously involved in multiple lawsuits, or is a large company that is constantly engaged in litigation.

For example, what if an employee transfers to a different department and now her documents are relevant to more than one lawsuit—when can you lift the litigation hold on her data be lifted? What if a company settles a securities class action lawsuit, but the Securities and Exchange Commission is still investigating the company over the same disclosures that were the subject of the class action? With regard to a litigation hold implemented in anticipation of litigation that never materializes, how long before the hold can be lifted? The decision to lift a litigation hold requires due diligence to ensure that the preserved data set is not relevant to any claims or defenses for other litigation matters, including audits or investigations.

H.   PRESERVATION ORDERS

In *Capricorn Power Co. v. Siemens Westinghouse Power Corp.*, 220 F.R.D. 429 (W.D. Pa. 2004), the court addressed the standard for issuing a preservation order. The court decided that a balancing test considering the following three factors should be used to decide whether to issue a preservation order: ''1) the level of concern the court has for the continuing existence and maintenance of the integrity of the evidence in question in the absence of an order directing preservation of the evidence; 2) any irreparable harm likely to result to the party seeking the preservation of evidence absent an order directing preservation; and 3) the capability of an individual, entity, or party to maintain the evidence sought to be preserved, not only as to the evidence's original form, condition or contents, but also the physical, spatial and financial burdens created by ordering evidence preservation.'' The court also noted that a motion for a preservation order can be granted as to all discoverable evidence, whether or not that evidence will be admissible at trial.

In discussing the first factor, the need to maintain the integrity of the evidence, the court pointed out that at times evidence may not be in the possession, custody or control of any of the parties. There may also be a concern that a party is intentionally damaging or destroying evidence, or is planning to do so. Finally, the parties may disagree as to the best way to preserve the integrity of the evidence. The court stated that the goal is to maintain the original evidence in the safest possible manner.

The second factor is the degree of the harm likely to result to the party seeking the preservation order. Some evidence can never be replicated and must be preserved at all costs. Some evidence may be so important to a party's case that a preservation order is warranted even in the absence of a threat of imminent or significant harm.

The third and final factor is the ease or difficulty of preserving the particular evidence. The court gave, as examples, consideration of storage space, maintenance and storage fees, and the physical deterioration of the evidence. The court noted that storage space concern is less of a consideration with respect to some ESI (CDs or USBs) than with paper records. Similarly, evidence stored within a computer hard drive may be difficult to preserve as new information is added and old information is deleted or overwritten. Applying its three-part test, the court denied requests from both parties to issue a preservation order with respect to the other party's records.

Aside from providing that parties should "discuss any issues about preserving discoverable information" early in the proceedings, the Federal Rules do not specify how relevant information should be preserved or how one litigant can ensure that the other will not destroy relevant information before it is produced in the course of litigation. In some cases, one or both parties may ask the court to enter a preservation order that will instruct a party to preserve certain types of information and dictate how it is to be preserved. It is important to remember, however, that a party's obligation to preserve relevant information exists even in the absence of such an order.

1.   Seeking a Preservation Order

A litigant requests a preservation order when it anticipates that its opponent may fail to comply with its preservation obligations. For example, a party may seek a preservation order against a party who has a history of discovery misconduct or spoliation violations, or whose routine operating procedures or document retention practices will likely result in destruction.

The inherently temporary or fleeting nature of certain types of information may also lead a party to seek a preservation order. In *Columbia Pictures Industries v. Bunnell*, cited earlier in this Chapter, plaintiffs claimed that discovery of the defendants' server's RAM was necessary in order to show how often users were downloading copyrighted movies. Because the RAM was overwritten every six hours, the plaintiffs sought a preservation order. After an extensive analysis, the court issued an order directing the defendants to maintain the server logs, which preserved the RAM.

Sometimes, the preserving party may itself have reasons to seek a preservation order. A court order that clearly defines and delimits a litigant's obligations could benefit the preserving party by potentially reducing its administrative and financial burdens. Additionally, if the preserving party faithfully complies with the court's order, the litigant may shield itself from future spoliation claims.

If discoverable information in the hands of a non-party custodian is at risk of being destroyed before production, a preservation notice and subpoena may be issued to the non-party. *In re Pacific Gateway Exchange, Inc. Securities Litigation,* 2001 WL 1334747 (N.D. Cal. Oct. 17, 2001), involved a defendant that had filed for Chapter 11 and was in bankruptcy proceedings. During this process, most of defendant's employees had left, and there were few personnel remaining to be responsible for preservation and production. Additionally, the court noted that there may be relevant data on former employees' personal computers. Finding a "significant risk that relevant documents, both paper and electronic, could be irretrievably lost, which could result in prejudice to plaintiffs," the court permitted the parties to serve a subpoena and notice to preserve documents to non-parties.

Similarly, *In re Tyco International, Ltd. Securities Litigation,* 2000 WL 33654141 (D.N.H. Jul. 27, 2000), was a multidistrict securities fraud litigation, in which the court agreed with plaintiffs that various non-parties, such as accountants, auditors, and consultants, could have possessed discoverable information about the transactions at issue. The court acknowledged that, unlike defendants, these non-parties had not necessarily received notice of the lawsuit. Moreover, plaintiffs had produced evidence showing that because these non-parties were large corporations, they would likely "overwrite and thereby destroy electronic data in the course of performing routine backup procedures." Accordingly, the court held that it would permit plaintiffs to serve preservation notices and subpoenas on these non-parties, provided that plaintiffs submitted revised, "appropriately tailored" subpoenas that particularized the types of evidence to be preserved.

2. Issuing a Preservation Order

Some courts have taken the approach of issuing a preservation order only where the standard for injunctive relief has been met. Courts applying the injunctive relief standard to a request for a preservation order generally require the requesting party to demonstrate potential irreparable injury and also show that there is a "real danger that the acts to be enjoined will occur, that there is no other remedy available, and that, under these circumstances, the court should exercise its discretion to afford the unusual relief provided by its injunction."[5]

Other courts have taken a different approach, recognizing a trial court's inherent power "to control the discovery process and overall case management" as a separate source of authority for issuing preservation orders. In *Pueblo of Laguna v. United States*, 60 Fed. Cl. 133 (2004), the court held that "a document preservation order is no more an injunction than an order requiring a party to identify witnesses or to produce documents in discovery." Drawing on its inherent power to manage the litigation before it, the court held that a preservation order should issue if the requesting party demonstrates "that it is necessary and not unduly burdensome."

In yet another variation, some courts, especially in complex cases, employ a standard, "first day" order at the start of the litigation that contains form language regarding the parties' preservation obligations.[6] For example, in some multidistrict liti-

5. *Humble Oil & Refining Co. v. Harang*, 262 F. Supp. 39 (E.D. La. 1966).

6. *See Manual for Complex Litigation* § 11.442 (4th ed. 2004) ("Before discovery starts, and perhaps before the initial conference, the court should consider whether to enter an order requir-

gation, the first order the court issues may automatically require all parties to preserve all documents and other records containing information potentially relevant to the subject matter of the litigation.

State courts have also begun to address preservation of ESI. In 2006, the Conference of Chief Justices released "Guidelines for State Trial Courts Regarding Discovery of Electronically–Stored Information." The Guidelines state that a trial court should only issue a preservation order upon "a threshold showing that the continuing existence and integrity of the information is threatened." Following a threshold showing, the Guidelines instruct trial courts to consider four factors—similar to those used in *Capricorn Power*—in fashioning an order: (1) the nature of the threat to the ESI; (2) the potential for irreparable harm without an order; (3) the responding party's ability to maintain the information sought; and (4) the physical, technological, and financial burdens in preserving the information.

3. Content and Scope of Preservation Orders

A preservation order should be narrowly tailored to the specific risks and needs of the case to avoid imposing unduly burdensome requirements on the parties. Because litigants know best what informa-

ing the parties to preserve and retain documents, files, data, and records that may be relevant to the litigation.").

tion is needed, where it is kept, and how it can most efficiently be preserved, a court may institute a general, temporary preservation order and instruct the litigants to meet and confer to develop a more detailed, customized preservation agreement. Such an order may also be useful if one party refuses to discuss in detail the issue of preservation. When ordered to meet and confer to develop a preservation plan, litigants should evaluate the following considerations:

- the extent of the preservation obligation, identifying the types of material to be preserved, the subject matter, time frame, the authors and addressees, and key words to be used in identifying responsive materials;

- the identification of persons responsible for carrying out preservation obligations on behalf of each party;

- the form and method of providing notice of the duty to preserve to persons identified as custodians of documents, data, and tangible things;

- mechanisms for monitoring, certifying, or auditing custodian compliance with preservation obligations;

- whether preservation will require suspending or modifying any routine business processes or procedures, with special attention to document management programs and the recycling of computer data storage media;

- the methods to preserve any volatile but potentially discoverable material, such as voicemail, active data in databases, or electronic messages;

- the anticipated costs of preservation and ways to reduce or share these costs; and

- a mechanism to review and modify the preservation obligation as discovery proceeds, eliminating or adding particular categories of documents, data, and tangible things.

I. POSSESSION, CUSTODY, OR CONTROL

In *In re NTL, Inc. Securities Litigation*, 244 F.R.D. 179 (S.D.N.Y. 2007), the court addressed the difficult question of whether records are in a party's possession, custody, or control and thus subject to a duty to preserve. The court began by noting that under Rule 34, "control does not require that the party have legal ownership or actual physical possession of the documents at issue; rather, documents are considered to be under a party's control when that party has the right, authority, or practical ability to obtain the documents from a nonparty to the action." Moreover, the court found that once the duty to preserve material for litigation arises a party has a duty to initiate a litigation hold and preserve potentially responsive documents and ESI. Once a party issued that hold notice it could not turn over those documents to another entity without preserving such information for possible production in litigation or ensuring that the entity to which records were transferred preserved the information.

The same issue was addressed in *Hatfill v. The New York Times Company*, 242 F.R.D. 353 (E.D. Va. 2006). In that case plaintiff sought a reporter's research and interview notes which were maintained on his personal flash drive. The court began by noting that control is defined as actual possession of a document or "the legal right to obtain the document on demand." The court concluded that defendant newspaper did not have physical possession of the flash drive containing the reporter's notes. In addition, the notes were not stored on any of defendant's computers. Finally, the court found that defendant had agreed that the unpublished notes would be retained by the reporter and did not belong to defendant. As a result, the court declined to compel defendant to produce the reporter's notes.

1. What Is Control?

It is important to recognize that Rules 26, 34, and 45 all have "possession, custody, or control" requirements. The requirement in Rule 26 is particularly important because it may create a trap. Under Rule 26, a party discloses documents in its "possession, custody, or control" on which it intends to affirmatively rely. Thus, a Rule 26 disclosure could be viewed as an admission that a party has "possession, custody, or control" over certain records, which may affect its responses to Rule 34 discovery demands.

a. The Practical Ability Test

The *In re NTL* court relied, in part, on the producing party's "practical ability" to obtain the documents in question. Whether a party's "practical ability" to obtain discovery materials means that a party has "control" over those materials has been the subject of some debate. In *Prokosch v. Catalina Lighting, Inc.*, 193 F.R.D. 633 (D. Minn. 2000), the court wrote: "[t]herefore, under Rule 34, 'control' does not require that the party have legal ownership or actual physical possession of the documents at issue; rather, documents are considered to be under a party's control when that party has the right, authority, or practical ability, to obtain the documents from a non-party to the action." The court ordered defendant to produce certain documents that it "may not physically possess, but which it is capable of obtaining upon demand."

The Seventh Circuit, however, rejected the practical ability test in *Chaveriat v. Williams Pipe Line Co.*, 11 F.3d 1420 (7th Cir. 1993), in overturning a trial court's decision to exclude certain evidence because plaintiffs failed to turn over chromatograms to defendant for more than two years. The chromatograms were in the possession of NET, a non-party, and plaintiffs ultimately asked for and received them from NET. After stating the "possession, custody, or control" requirement, the court wrote:

> The plaintiffs could no doubt have asked NET
> to give it the chromatograms; judging from

what happened later, NET would have complied; and maybe if it had balked, the plaintiffs could have bought the chromatograms from it. But the fact that a party could obtain a document if it tried hard enough and maybe if it didn't try hard at all does not mean that the document is in its possession, custody, or control; in fact it means the opposite.

Similarly, in *Bleecker v. Standard Fire Insurance Co.*, 130 F. Supp. 2d 726 (E.D.N.C. 2000), the court also rejected the practical ability test. The issue involved documents in the possession of a non-party insurance adjuster. Plaintiff asserted that defendant had the ability to "command" the documents. The court wrote:

> Plaintiff's and Defendant's definitions of control differ greatly. Plaintiff asserts that even if a party does not have the right to require a non-party to produce documents, the party's practical *ability* to produce the documents determines whether the defendant has "control" of the document. On the other hand, defendant contends that "control" encompasses the legal *right* to obtain the requested document.

The court agreed with the defendant: "In order for the material to be discoverable, defendant must have some type of legal right to the material plaintiff seeks to discover."

b. Party and Non-Party Data Stores

Obviously, the parties to litigation have an obligation to preserve relevant evidence, including ESI, as soon as the duty to preserve arises. Even before being formally named in a complaint, a person or entity that reasonably anticipates *becoming a party* to future litigation has a duty to preserve.

But what are the obligations of parties to preserve relevant information they know is held by non-parties? This question is particularly important in the context of ESI. Today, many businesses out source their IT needs, both maintaining day-to-day electronic data on servers owned and operated by non-party hosts and storing long-term inactive data, such as disaster recovery backup tapes and other archival data with vendors providing off-site storage.

In addition to evidence over which a party has direct care, custody or control, the duty to preserve may extend to evidence over which a party has indirect control. For example, In *Cyntegra, Inc. v. Idexx Laboratories*, cited earlier in this Chapter, plaintiff stored most of its electronic data on non-party servers run by a vendor, NetNation. Because plaintiff was delinquent on payments to NetNation, the vendor deleted plaintiff's data from its servers. In sanctioning plaintiff for NetNation's destruction of the evidence, the court held that:

> Plaintiff had sufficient control and legal right over the deleted files to constitute fault. Plain-

tiff contracted to store business documents on NetNation's computer servers. At least until ... payment was discontinued, Plaintiff could direct the flow of information to and from NetNation's servers. Because [Plaintiff's duty to preserve had already arisen at the time payment was discontinued], it had an affirmative duty to make payments and preserve the evidence. Plaintiff cannot bypass this duty by abandoning its documents to a third-party and claiming lack of control. Plaintiff could have saved or printed the information after determining it could no longer make payments. . . . A contractual relationship with a third-party entity provides, at a minimum, an obligation to make reasonable inquiry of the third-party entity for the data at issue. . . . Plaintiff had sufficient, albeit indirect, control to preserve evidence, and by failing to do so, violated an affirmative duty.

c.   Parent, Subsidiary, and Affiliate Corporations

Courts generally hold that a parent corporation has a sufficient degree of ownership and control over a wholly-owned subsidiary such that the parent is deemed to have control over the subsidiary's documents. Courts have applied this principle even when the parent corporation does not own the subsidiary directly, but rather when an intermediate corporation that is itself a wholly-owned subsidiary of the parent corporation owns the subsidiary.

In *Alcan International Ltd. v. S.A. Day Manufacturing Co.*, 176 F.R.D. 75 (W.D.N.Y. 1996), the court ordered a U.S. corporate defendant to produce documents in the possession of its foreign affiliate. The court stated that the U.S. and foreign companies "are corporate members of a unified worldwide business entity," issue consolidated financial statements, use the same corporate logo, and have regular contact regarding the issues in the case. The court wrote: "It is 'inconceivable' that [defendant] would not have access to this information and the ability to obtain it, not only for the purpose of proving its claims in this lawsuit but also for the purpose of conducting its business...."

The court reached a different result in *Goh v. Baldor Electric Co.*, 1999 WL 20943 (N.D. Tex. Jan. 13, 1999), where plaintiffs sought to compel Ernst & Young LLP to produce documents from Ernst & Young Singapore and Ernst & Young Thailand in a dispute involving events that took place in Asia. The court found that plaintiffs failed to meet their burden of showing control because the three companies, while part of a common association, operated separately. Ernst & Young Singapore and Ernst & Young Thailand "refused to turn over documents to Ernst & Young LLP in Dallas because it has a policy against voluntarily providing documents to be used in litigation." The court ruled: "[W]here Ernst & Young's foreign entities have refused to voluntarily provide the documents in question, it necessarily follows that Ernst & Young LLP in Dallas does not have control over the documents."

d.   Control Imposed by Law

Control may be imposed by law. *Tomlinson v. El Paso Corp.*, 245 F.R.D. 474 (D. Colo. 2007), involved claims that the employer's actions relating to a pension plan violated ERISA. Plaintiffs sought discovery of certain data from a non-party benefits administrator, and the employer claimed that it neither possessed nor controlled the data and, therefore, could not produce them. The court rejected the employer's argument. U.S. Department of Labor regulations applying to ERISA plans required that the employer maintain the data that plaintiffs sought. The court wrote:

> ERISA imposes upon the Defendants the duty to ensure that the "recordkeeping system has reasonable controls" such that its employee benefits records are "accessible ... in such a manner as they may be readily inspected or examined." ... Defendants cannot delegate their duties to a third party under ERISA. ... Consequently, Defendants are in possession, custody or control over the requested data ... such that they have, or should have, the authority and ability to obtain the requested data.

e.   Control Based on Agency

Corporations may have a legal right to obtain documents from their agents. In *City of Seattle v. Professional Basketball Club, LLC*, 2008 WL 539809 (W.D. Wash. Feb. 25, 2008), plaintiff sought the production of documents, including e-mails, from members of the limited liability corporation. The court stated:

> Here, the question is whether the City has met its burden in establishing that PBC has a legal right to obtain documents from its members. That question turns on whether a principal-agent relationship exists between PBC and its members....

Applying Oklahoma law, the court examined the operating agreement applicable to PBC and determined that each member was a "manager" under Oklahoma law. The court concluded: "Because a manager is an agent ... the requisite principal-agent relationship exists to establish that PBC has the legal right to obtain documents upon demand from its members."

f.   Outside Directors

Most major U.S. corporations have outside directors as part of their boards. These directors may have material responsive to production requests. Do corporations have an obligation to preserve documents in the hands of outside directors, who are deliberately separate from the corporation? In *In re Triton Energy Limited Securities Litigation*, 2002 WL 32114464 (E.D. Tex. Mar. 7, 2002), Triton did not inform its outside directors to preserve documents. Triton argued that it only had control over its employees and the documents within the employees' possession, and the outside directors were not employees. The court never answered the question of control, but instead stated: "The Court is of the opinion that it would have been prudent and within the spirit of the law for Triton to instruct its officers and directors to preserve and produce any documents in their possession, custody, or control."

g. Control Over Non-Party Service Providers

In *Columbia Pictures Industries v. Bunnell*, cited earlier in this Chapter, defendants contracted with Panther, a non-party service provider, to serve as a middleman for people trying to access defendants' web site. Plaintiffs sought server log data from defendants—data that were in Panther's possession. The Magistrate Judge concluded that defendants controlled the server log data:

> The record reflects that defendants have the ability to manipulate at will how the Server Log Data is routed. Consequently, the court concludes that even though the Server Log Data is now routed to Panther and is temporarily stored in Panther's RAM, the data remains in defendants' possession, custody or control.

On appeal, the district court agreed with the Magistrate Judge's conclusion that defendants controlled the server log data because they had the ability to reroute the Server Log Data through their own servers.

In *Keir v. Unumprovident Corp.*, 2003 WL 21997747 (S.D.N.Y. Aug. 22, 2003), defendant failed to take the necessary steps to preserve backup tapes in the possession of a non-party vendor. Plaintiffs sought the production of e-mails, which required defendant to preserve certain backup tapes maintained by IBM, a non-party vendor. Various errors and missteps resulted in the loss of certain potentially relevant e-mails. While the court ultimately ruled that the mistakes were the "fault of no one," the court found that defendant failed to consult with IBM to ensure that the relevant backup tapes were preserved.

2.   What Is Possession?

This question was addressed in *Phillips v. Netblue, Inc.*, 2007 WL 174459 (N.D. Cal. Jan. 22, 2007), an interesting case in which defendant moved to sanction a plaintiff for failing to produce relevant information. The court stated that it could not consider a sanction unless it determined that plaintiff had a duty to preserve the now-missing information. In order to determine whether plaintiff had that duty the court analyzed whether the missing information was ever in plaintiff's possession. The information at issue consisted of images that could be accessed through hyperlinks found in e-mails received by plaintiff, as well as advertisements accessed through the hyperlinks. The problem raised in the case was that the images could no longer be obtained and the advertisements were no longer accessible. Had plaintiff opened each e-mail containing a hyperlink and maintained the image accessed through the hyperlink and had it maintained the URLs at which each advertisement could be found, then defendant could have reviewed this information.

The court began its analysis by noting that plaintiff was not accused of destroying the actual e-mails but rather of not "memorializing" the e-mails as they would have appeared on the date of receipt—namely with the images and addresses obtained through the hyperlinks. The court swiftly rejected defendant's argument holding that a party has no obligation to keep that which it never had. Plaintiff kept the e-mails. What it did not do was keep the information that could have been reached through following the steps on the hyperlinks. The court found that plaintiff was never in possession of this information. The court concluded that defendant was faulting plaintiff for failing to "gather" evidence, not for failing to "preserve" it.

a. Opportunity   to   Possess/Functional Control

In *In re WRT Energy Securities Litigation*, 246 F.R.D. 185 (S.D.N.Y. 2007), the court held that a party had a duty to preserve documents which it had been given an opportunity to possess but declined. In that case, as a result of a bankruptcy, Gulfport, a non-party, acquired 1,100 boxes of documents that were being preserved as part of ongoing litigation. After the parties in the securities fraud case had reviewed the documents, Gulfport's general counsel notified the parties that it intended to destroy the documents because it would be leasing the warehouse in which they were being stored. None of the parties objected to Gulfport disposing of the documents.

After the documents had been destroyed, plaintiffs disclosed, for the first time, that their expert would be opining on additional topics, and defendants objected because it no longer had access to the documents to refute plaintiffs' expert's new opinions. The court held that plaintiffs had an obligation to preserve the documents that were relevant to previously undisclosed expert topics despite the fact that plaintiffs neither had custody of the documents nor destroyed them. The court wrote:

> In the instant case, the plaintiffs . . . had functional control of the Gulfport documents since they were advised that the documents would be destroyed and were given the opportunity to take custody of them. Therefore, the preservation obligation attached.

As a result of plaintiffs' failure to preserve the documents, the court ruled that plaintiffs could not contest key issues at trial, that defendants would receive an adverse inference instruction, and that plaintiffs must pay for defendants' attorneys' fees associated with the motion as well as for new analyses that defendants' expert had to perform.

b. Access Alone Does Not Equal Possession

In *In re Kuntz*, 124 S.W.3d 179 (Tex. 2003), the Texas Supreme Court ruled, in a divorce proceeding, that access alone does not equal possession. In an effort to enforce a settlement agreement, the wife sought discovery about royalty payments to which the husband was entitled. MOXY (an oil company) owned the documents that CLK, a consulting firm in which the husband was a manager and minority owner, possessed. Additionally, the documents contained trade secrets and the consulting agreement between MOXY and CLK obligated CLK to maintain the confidentiality of the documents.

The husband asserted that "in his individual capacity, he does not have physical possession of the requested documents and has no legal right to obtain the documents from either CLK or MOXY." The wife argued the opposite, stating that the "testimony in this case was unequivocal that the [documents] were in the [husband's] offices and he could get them anytime he wants." The Texas Supreme Court agreed with the husband:

> [Husband], an employee of CLK, lacks both physical possession of MOXY's trade secret [documents] or any "right to possess" MOXY's trade secret [documents]. At best, all [husband] has is access to MOXY's trade secret [documents] and that access is strictly limited to use

of the [documents] in furtherance of his employer's services performed for MOXY. Like a bank teller with access to cash in the vault, [husband] has neither possession nor any right to possess MOXY's trade secret [documents].

c. Possession Does Not Require Ownership

Actual possession, not ownership, determines whether a party must produce documents. In *In re Bankers Trust Co.*, 61 F.3d 465 (6th Cir. 1995), a bank claimed that it could not produce documents in its possession because the Federal Reserve had provided the documents to the bank and maintained ownership over the documents. The court rejected the argument, stating that the bank was in "actual possession" of the documents and that "legal ownership . . . is not determinative."

The bank also claimed that it could not produce the documents because a federal regulation forbade the bank from doing so. The court also rejected this argument. While recognizing that "federal regulations should be adhered to and given full force . . . whenever possible," the court found that the Federal Reserve, which promulgated the regulation in question, did not have "the power to promulgate federal regulations in direct contravention of the Federal Rules of Civil Procedure." The court concluded, "Congress did not empower the Federal Reserve to prescribe regulations that direct a party to deliberately disobey a court order, subpoena, or other judicial mechanism requiring the production of information."

Similarly, in *United States v. National Broadcasting Co.*, 65 F.R.D. 415 (C.D. Cal. 1974), a dispute arose over former President Nixon's documents. The court wrote: "It must be noted that any determinations made by this Court regarding the motions before it does not involve the question of 'ownership' of former President Nixon's documents. What is involved here is the 'possession, custody and control' of these documents."

CHAPTER III

MEET AND CONFER (RULE 26(f)) AND INITIAL SCHEDULING CONFERENCE (RULE 16)

A. THE RULE 26(f) CONFERENCE

Rule 26(f) requires attorneys to meet before the Rule 16 scheduling order is due, and discuss four new topics. The Rule forces parties to focus on the problems of preservation and e-discovery on the front end of a litigation instead of potentially facing sanctions motions on the back end for failure to preserve and/or produce information.

Attorneys are now expected to learn where and how the client's records are maintained (remembering that the duty to disclose applies to records in a party's "possession, custody or control"). They should also be prepared to discuss issues of cost and accessibility at the outset of the case. Finally, attorneys should identify at this early stage what is really at issue in a case because unfocused discovery means uncontrollable costs.

The four new topics the attorneys are to address at the 26(f) conference are: (1) the preservation of evidence (with a focus on electronic records); (2) the discovery or disclosure of ESI; (3) the form that the production will take; and (4) a procedure for retrieving inadvertently produced privileged information. In addressing these issues attorneys have a duty to cooperate in order to achieve the just and speedy resolution of the case.

The meet and confer obligation raises some difficult questions. The most important concern is how much can the parties expect to accomplish in the initial meet and confer. Would the parties be wise to consider the meet and confer obligation to be a continuing process, with the parties agreeing to work on a cooperative basis, over a period of time and a series of meetings, to reduce the costs of discovery and focus on the real issues in a case? A key question to be addressed at all Rule 26(f) conferences is what needs to be preserved and what can be destroyed (*i.e.*, scope of preservation). One suggestion is that parties should agree on the sampling of data to learn more about both the cost of review and production and the yield rate in terms of locating relevant information. This, in turn, might affect the decision as to the scope of preservation. Surely, the parties should consider whether some or all metadata must be produced. Some cases may call for some types of metadata to be produced, others may call for the production of different metadata, and some may not require the production of any metadata at all. This is a case-specific consideration. A final question that should be addressed is who should attend the meet and confer. As discussed below, a party may wish to bring a technical consultant to the Rule 26(f) conference in cases where a large quantity of ESI is stored in many different locations and formats.

1. Preservation of Evidence

With respect to the preservation of evidence, the parties should strive to reach a rational agreement on what must be preserved, taking into account the costs and burden incurred by modifying or suspending whatever document retention system is in place in order to implement a litigation hold. The Advisory Committee Note expressly discourages courts from entering blanket preservation orders and suggests that any preservation order be narrowly tailored. A court should only enter a preservation order when it is concerned that evidence may disappear or when the party seeking the order will be irreparably harmed if evidence disappears.

An interesting question that courts have addressed is whether a party must produce its internally-distributed document retention protocol and/or its litigation hold notice. Three recent decisions have all held that these notices need not be produced because they are privileged. A fourth case held that the notice need not be produced because it constitutes attorney work product.

On the other hand, in *In re eBay Seller Antitrust Litigation,* 2007 WL 2852364 (N.D. Cal. Oct. 2, 2007), a Magistrate Judge found that although the notice itself was privileged, plaintiff was permitted to discover the names of all six hundred employees to whom the notice was sent and "the facts regard-

ing defendant's retention and collection policies."
In *Wells v. Xpedx*, 2007 WL 1200955 (M.D. Fla. Apr.
23, 2007), the court permitted a party's representative to be deposed on the topic of the company's e-
mail retention policy. Finally, in *In re Grand Jury
Investigation*, 445 F.3d 266 (3d Cir. 2006), an appellate court held that a company's failure to halt the
systematic deletion of e-mail after receiving a subpoena, entitled the government to review e-mail
correspondence as well as notes from company
counsel to the company's executive director based
on the crime-fraud exception to the attorney client
privilege.

A second issue implicating the duty to preserve is
identifying those records within a party's possession, custody or control. Such records include: (a)
current and archived records; (b) records of current
employees and former employees; (c) records of
acquired companies and spin-offs, (d) records of
bankrupt entities that may have migrated; and (e)
records stored off-site or by non-parties (*e.g.*, ISPs
or vendors).

These five categories of records raise many difficult issues. We have chosen to highlight a few. The
first is the blurring of the distinction between personal and business e-mail and therefore between
work and home computers. Many people maintain
two e-mail accounts—a business account and a personal account. But most people do not strictly limit
their use of their business e-mail account to business, nor their use of their personal account to
personal correspondence. Because of this, issues of

preservation, production, and privilege waiver have arisen with respect to both business and personal e-mail.

In *Easton Sports, Inc. v. Warrior LaCrosse, Inc.*, 2006 WL 2811261 (E.D. Mich. Sept. 28, 2006), a trade secrets case involving an employee who allegedly took customer lists and other proprietary information to his new employer, the court sanctioned the new employer for the employee's destruction of e-mail in his personal e-mail account. The court held that the employer negligently failed to preserve relevant evidence from its employee—including evidence found in a personal e-mail account—stating that defendant "should have done more to detect and preserve relevant data under [the employee's] control." In *Ameriwood Industries, Inc. v. Liberman*, 2006 WL 3825291 (E.D. Mo. Dec. 27, 2006), another recent trade secrets case, the court allowed a neutral expert to inspect the personal computers of defendant's employees because the employer had failed to produce e-mails that non-party customers had previously produced. Additionally, it is now well settled that an employee's use of a corporate computer to transmit or receive privileged communications waives the privilege when the employee is on notice that the employer reserves the right to review the communications.

What if records are in a party's control but not in its possession? This topic is discussed in Chapter II, *supra*. Nonetheless, this topic is also important in the context of the Rule 26(f) conference because the duty to preserve can only cover evidence that is in a party's possession, custody or control. A couple examples may be helpful. In *Tomlinson v. El Paso Corp.*, 245 F.R.D. 474 (D. Colo. 2007), an ERISA action, the court held that although a non-party possessed the records plaintiff sought, the records were effectively in defendant's custody and control because defendant had a duty under ERISA to maintain the data for inspection and examination. However, in *Modern Engineering v. Peterson*, 2007 WL 2680563 (C.D. Ill. July 16, 2007), plaintiff sued its former employee for stealing proprietary information and giving it to his new employer, and sought all records that defendant had "transmitted" or "presented" to his new employer. The court held that those records that "belonged" to the new employer were not in defendant's control, but required production of any records that remained in defendant's custody. The court also noted that plaintiff had available means, other than defendant, through which those documents could be obtained.

2.   Discovery or Disclosure of ESI

The second new topic for the Rule 26(f) conference is the discovery or disclosure of ESI. The Advisory Committee Note suggests that early discovery from persons with special knowledge of a company's computer systems, by way of deposition, interrogatory, or questionnaire may be particularly useful. Attorneys should identify the sources in which relevant information is stored; the time period at issue; the key players; a rational search proto-

col (agreeing on key word search terms for example); the accessibility of information; and the cost
and burden of restoring information that is not
reasonably accessible.

3.   Form of Production

The third topic attorneys must discuss is the form
in which they want information produced—paper or
electronic production is the first question, and if
electronic then whether the format will be native,
TIFF, PDF, searchable, and whether it will include
metadata. To discuss this topic intelligently it is
important to distinguish among different kinds of
metadata, which is covered in Chapter V, *infra*.

4.   Retrieving Privileged Information

The fourth topic on which parties must confer is
the procedure for retrieving privileged information
that has been inadvertently produced in the course
of discovery ("claw back") or alternatively, they
should discuss whether they will agree to initially
forgo any review without waiving privilege ("quick
peek"). If they reach an agreement they should
request that the court incorporate the agreement in
an order. The recent passage of Rule 502 of the
Federal Rules of Evidence, discussed at length in
Chapter VIII, *infra*, will now be an important part
of any discussion at the Rule 26(f) conference with
respect to privilege issues.

5. Duty to Cooperate

In *In re Bristol–Myers Squibb Securities Litigation*, 205 F.R.D. 437 (D.N.J. 2002), the court noted that "lawyers try cases, not judges," and placed on the attorneys' shoulders the burden of cooperatively preparing an electronic discovery plan:

> [Rule] 26(f) provides that before a Rule 16 Conference, the parties "confer . . . to develop a proposed discovery plan. . . ." In the electronic age, this meet and confer should include a discussion on whether each side possesses information in electronic form, whether they intend to produce such material, whether each other's software is compatible . . . and how to allocate costs involved with each of the foregoing. [Local Rule] 26(b)(2) addresses the requirements of [Federal Rule] 26(f) and, in addition, requires parties to discuss any "special procedure." Moreover, the standard initial scheduling order in this District contains instructions on topics to be discussed in the preparation of a Joint Discovery Plan which include "(3) a description of all discovery problems encountered to date, the efforts undertaken by the parties to remedy these problems, and the parties' suggested resolution of problems; [and] (4) a description of the parties' further discovery needs." Although there may be room for clearer direction in existing rules and orders that explicitly address cost allocation in production of paper and electronic information, counsel should take advantage of the required Rule 26(f) meeting to discuss issues associated with electronic discovery.

Because electronic discovery consultants are often hired to assist attorneys in retrieving, preserving, and producing electronic information, it might be wise to have these consultants participate in the Rule 26(f) meet and confer process in order to have meaningful discussions about electronic discovery issues.

Finally, the Sedona Conference and several courts have urged counsel to adopt a more cooperative, less adversarial stance at the initial meet and confer. In the summer of 2008, the Conference issued its "Cooperation Proclamation"—endorsed by many judges—exhorting lawyers to "strive in the best interests of their clients to achieve the best results at a reasonable cost, with integrity and candor as officers of the court." Lawyers are urged to work cooperatively at the Rule 26(f) conference to identify at an early stage all issues relating to electronic discovery including, presumably, issues relating to preservation, search terms and forms of production. A number of courts have already cited to the Cooperation Proclamation and have noted that cooperation is a professional obligation. *See, e.g., Mancia v. Mayflower Textile Services Co.*, 253 F.R.D. 354 (D. Md. 2008). *See also* Chapter VII, *infra.*

B. THE RULE 16 CONFERENCE

Rule 16(a) permits, but does not require, a court to order the attorneys to appear for a pretrial conference for several purposes—two of which are particularly important in the context of the discovery. The first, Rule 16(a)(2) speaks of "establishing early and continuing control so that the case will not be protracted because of lack of management" and the second, Rule 16(a)(3) suggests that courts "discourag[e] wasteful pretrial activities." Rule 16(b) requires the court to issue a scheduling order that includes provisions for the disclosure or discovery of ESI and the parties' agreement, if any, for asserting privilege or protection claims after production.

C. THE INTERPLAY BETWEEN RULE 26(f) AND RULE 16

The meet and confer(s) required by Rule 26(f) work in conjunction with the parties' Rule 16 pretrial conference with the court. Specifically, Rule 26(f)(1) requires the parties to meet and confer to develop a proposed discovery plan prior to the Rule 16 pretrial conference, typically scheduled by the court at the outset of the litigation for the purpose of creating a scheduling order for discovery and other pretrial matters. After the Rule 26(f) meet and confer, the parties must submit a written report to the court outlining a proposed discovery plan for the litigation. At the Rule 16 pretrial conference, the parties meet with the court to discuss, among other matters, the proposed discovery schedule and any anticipated discovery disputes. After the Rule 16 conference, the court issues a scheduling order, generally based in part on the parties' report, containing deadlines that will govern the timing of discovery and, potentially, provisions relating to the retrieval and production of ESI. The Rule 26(f) discovery conference is not merely a perfunctory exercise. Rather, it is an opportunity for the parties to educate themselves and their adversaries, anticipate and resolve electronic discovery disputes before they escalate, expedite the progress of their case, and assess and manage litigation costs. As a matter of strategy, the Rule 26(f) discovery conference provides the parties an opportunity to prepare themselves for the Rule 16 pretrial conference, so that they can demonstrate to the court that they have made diligent, good faith efforts to comply with the Rules and the court's policies and therefore deserve the court's confidence.

The obligation to address electronic discovery at the Rule 26(f) meet and confer rests with the litigants. The 2006 Amendments do not *require* judges to address electronic discovery in the Rule 16 scheduling order. Perhaps due to this flexibility, the attention courts pay to litigants' meet and confer obligations varies widely across jurisdictions and from judge to judge. This may seem surprising given the ubiquity of electronic discovery disputes, but a survey of the relevant case law yields opinions that focus on electronic discovery in widely varying degrees. Likewise, some jurisdictions have promulgated local rules containing exhaustive lists of topics to be addressed by the parties at a Rule 26(f) meet and confer, while others limit their treatment of the issue to a simple verbatim recitation of Rule 26(f).

The importance of the Rule 26(f) meet and confer is indirectly underscored by Rule 16(f)(1)(B), which authorizes a court to impose sanctions on a party or its attorney if either "is substantially unprepared to participate—or does not participate in good faith— in the [Rule 16 pretrial] conference." Although the 2006 Amendments did not directly affect this provision, it incorporates by reference revised portions of Rules 16 and 26 that address electronic discovery, effectively holding litigants to a higher standard of preparedness with regard to electronic discovery matters by subjecting them to a risk of sanctions for failure to sufficiently prepare for the Rule 16 pretrial conference.

The Rule 26(f) meet and confer requirement facilitates the early identification of electronic discovery issues in order to prevent expensive and time-consuming discovery disputes. Once identified, the parties must be prepared to discuss any potentially problematic electronic discovery issues at the Rule 16 pretrial conference. The Advisory Committee Note to Rule 16 discusses the interplay between the two rules:

> The amendment to Rule 16(b) is designed to alert the court to the possible need to address the handling of discovery of electronically stored information early in the litigation if such discovery is expected to occur. Rule 26(f) is

amended to direct the parties to discuss discovery of electronically stored information if such discovery is contemplated in the action.... In many instances, the court's involvement early in the litigation will help avoid difficulties that might otherwise arise.

D. THE RESULTS OF FAILING TO COOPERATE AT THE 26(f) CONFERENCE

The decision in *In re Seroquel Products Liability Litigation*, 244 F.R.D. 650 (M.D. Fla. 2007), shows what can happen when the parties fail to effectively engage in the meet and confer process. This case arose in the context of a multi-district pharmaceutical products liability case. After plaintiffs repeatedly failed to obtain discovery, they sought court assistance. After exhaustively reviewing the history of failed discovery, the court found that defendant had engaged in "purposeful sluggishness." Sanctionable conduct included producing ESI without necessary metadata; producing non-searchable multi-page TIFF images, some consisting of more than twenty thousand pages; producing electronic documents without apparent Bates numbering; producing eight percent of the entire production as one lengthy document which could only be opened with a very powerful work station; and producing electronic files with no load files, rendering the production inaccessible and unusable. In addition, defendant employed a "plainly inadequate" key word search methodology "in secret" to cull responsive documents from the collections of eighty custodians, instead of engaging in a cooperative process with plaintiff, and did not cooperate in good faith to identify responsive databases. The court noted that these and other technical problems "likely could have been resolved far sooner and less expensively had [defendant] cooperated by fostering consultation between the technical staffs responsible for production. Instead, [defendant] shielded its non-party technical contractor from all contact with Plaintiffs."

The court wrote that "particularly in complex litigation, there is a heightened need for the parties to confer about the format of the electronic discovery being produced." The court specifically noted that Rule 26(f) requires the parties to discuss any issues relating to the discovery of ESI including the form of production. In reviewing defendant's conduct of discovery the court found that defendant had failed to "make a sincere effort to facilitate an understanding of what records are kept and what their availability might be," failed to consult with plaintiffs regarding the use of "comprehensive search terms and methods," and "fail[ed] to cooperate in identification leading to appropriate production of its relevant databases."

The *Seroquel* case provides one example of a party's failure to live up to a court's Rule 16 expectations. Almost a year before writing the *Seroquel* opinion, the Magistrate Judge admonished the parties for failing to resolve their discovery and scheduling issues through the meet and confer process.

Significantly, the Magistrate Judge noted that he was "flabbergasted as to how unprepared the parties [were]." Though neither party was sanctioned under Rule 16(f)(1)(B), the court's disappointments with the parties' pretrial conduct caused it to lose confidence in them, and its frustration with their conduct weighed heavily against them at later stages in the litigation.

In determining that sanctions were warranted for discovery abuse in *Seroquel*, the court analyzed the whole of the discovery process leading up to the parties' dispute. The parties' efforts to meet and confer made up a very important part of this larger examination. Thus when attorneys engage in meet and confers and other electronic discovery activities they should anticipate that the court may eventually scrutinize these activities. For this reason a litigant may choose to make a written record (a memo to file) of the meet and confer process. Moreover, the court criticized defendant for shielding its electronic discovery consultant from contact with plaintiffs. Significantly, the court argued that this failure to include knowledgeable electronic discovery consultants in the meet and confer is "antithetical to the Sedona Principles and is not an indicium of good faith."

Seroquel demonstrates that ESI's various volume, formatting, readability, and searchability issues can present difficult problems for litigants, potentially creating time-consuming and expensive discovery disputes. Consequently, courts increasingly interpret Rule 26 to require the parties to cooperate and communicate to avoid these potential problems. The 2006 Amendments to Rule 26 have impliedly removed the adversarial element from the Rule 26(f) discovery conference. As the *Seroquel* court noted, "identifying relevant records and working out technical methods for their production is a cooperative undertaking, not part of the adversarial give and take." Until recently counsel often treated discovery as just another phase in the adversarial process. Things have clearly changed. Rule 26 now encourages cooperation and transparency in electronic discovery practices.

E. LOCAL RULES OR COURT GUIDELINES

The 2006 Amendments' explicit reference to the importance of discussing electronic discovery issues during the Rule 26(f) meet and confer prompted many courts to revise their local rules. For instance, the United States District Courts for the District of Maryland and the District of Kansas have implemented detailed local rules governing electronic discovery.

State court judges have also devised electronic discovery guidelines. In 2006, the Conference of Chief Justices recommended that, following an initial discovery hearing or conference, a judge "should inquire whether counsel have reached agreement on [a variety of electronic discovery issues] and address any disputes."[1]

1. *See* Guidelines for State Trial Courts Regarding Discovery of Electronically Stored Information, at 654.

In *O'Bar v. Lowe's Home Centers, Inc.*, 2007 WL 1299180 (W.D.N.C. May 2, 2007), the court provided the parties lengthy and detailed "guidelines" to follow during and after their Rule 26(f) meet and confer. For example, the court directed the parties to meet and confer on the following issues, among others:

A. The anticipated scope of requests for, and objections to, production of ESI, as well as the form of production of ESI and, specifically, but without limitation, whether production will be of the Native File, Static Image, or other searchable or non-searchable formats.

B. Whether Meta-Data is requested for some or all ESI and, if so, the volume and costs of producing and reviewing said ESI.

C. Preservation of ESI during the pendency of the lawsuit, specifically, but without limitation, applicability of the "safe harbor" provision of Fed. R. Civ. P. 37, preservation of Meta-Data, preservation of deleted ESI, back up or archival ESI, ESI contained in dynamic systems, ESI destroyed or overwritten by the routine operation of systems, and, offsite and offline ESI (including ESI stored on home or personal computers). This discussion should include whether the parties can agree on methods of review of ESI by the responding party in a manner that does not unacceptably change Meta-Data.

* * *

E. Identification of ESI that is or is not reasonably accessible without undue burden or cost, specifically, and without limitation, the identity of such sources and the reasons for a contention that the ESI is or is not reasonably accessible without undue burden or cost, the methods of storing and retrieving that ESI, and the anticipated costs and efforts involved in retrieving that ESI. The party asserting that ESI is not reasonably accessible without undue burden or cost should be prepared to discuss in reasonable detail the basis for such assertion.

The litigants were required to follow the guidelines whenever possible and the guidelines would be "considered by the Court in resolving discovery disputes, including whether sanctions should be awarded pursuant to Fed. R. Civ. P. 37."

CHAPTER IV

DATA COLLECTION

Discovery of ESI involves the identification and collection of information from complex systems. Even relatively small organizations may have relevant ESI found on applications and databases, digital business and personal devices, and disks or tapes. Larger organizations may have network servers, shared drives, corporate intranets, stored archival data, disaster recovery backups, and data held by ISPs.

All sources that may contain responsive information must be identified and searched. It is also important that all counsel work together to ensure that all responsive information is collected. Outside counsel must acquire the necessary skills to understand the technical aspects of their clients' data. This may require the assistance of a technical or forensic computer expert. For example, terms such as "legacy data," "rollover servers," and "partitioned drives" have not been the traditional discovery fare of outside counsel. Nonetheless, a failure to understand these technical concepts has resulted in the imposition of sanctions based on counsel's failure to explain why responsive information was never collected.

In *Peskoff v. Faber*, 2006 WL 1933483 (D.D.C. July 11, 2006), plaintiff moved to compel further production of e-mails it claimed were missing from defendant's prior production. Defense counsel represented that it "caused the creation of an archive of all Peskoff electronic files, including documents stored on his computer hard drive, e-mail, and any other Peskoff electronic documents," and that this entire archive was produced to plaintiff. Noting that "[t]his statement tells me little, if anything about the scope of [defendant's] search," the judge enumerated five potential sources of relevant e-mail, ordering that defendant file a detailed affidavit within ten business days specifying the nature of the search it conducted, adding that after reviewing the affidavit, the court may hold an evidentiary hearing and take testimony about the effectiveness and cost of additional searches.

In *Phoenix Four, Inc. v. Strategic Resources Corp.*, 2006 WL 1409413 (S.D.N.Y. May 23, 2006), outside counsel was sanctioned when plaintiff discovered on the eve of trial that relevant data residing on a partitioned section of defendant's server had not been located or produced. The court roundly criticized counsel for failing to interrogate the client fully regarding its information systems. The court noted:

Further, [counsel's] obligation under *Zubulake V* extends to an inquiry as to whether information was stored on that server and, had the defendants been unable to answer that question, directing that a technician examine the server.

Outside counsel, together with in-house counsel, are responsible for performing an adequate data collection, and may be liable for any failure to do so. There are times when outside counsel must direct in-house counsel and other employees within a company to examine sources of information that they might otherwise overlook. Counsel might also be required to test the accuracy of a client's response to document demands to be sure that all appropriate sources of data have been searched and that responsive information has been collected and eventually reviewed and produced. And it is always wise to document the steps taken to collect responsive ESI.

Questionnaires and checklists are helpful tools to plan, execute, and document the data-collection process. The following checklists are adapted from Hon. Shira A. Scheindlin & Jonathan M. Redgrave, *Ch. 22: Discovery of Electronic Information, in Business and Commercial Litigation in Federal Courts 2d* (Robert L. Haig, ed., rev. ed. 2008).

A. INTERVIEWS OF VARIOUS EMPLOYEES

The following checklists are intended as a guide to assist counsel in identifying the existence and location of potentially relevant ESI. The lists, by their very nature, are both over-inclusive and under-inclusive. In particular, the facts and circumstances of any given case will dictate the nature and extent of preservation and production obligations, and the necessary level of due diligence. With that caveat, counsel should review these possible topics to determine which matters must be explored.

1. Initial Steps

- Identify records likely to be relevant to the claims and defenses in the litigation.

- Identify employees likely to have knowledge and information relevant to the subject matter of the litigation.

- Identify information services ("IS") personnel (which can be difficult because the organization of information services departments varies among companies, and, tends to change frequently given the dynamic nature of computing technology).

- Identify hardware support group personnel.

- Identify the group responsible for system maintenance, backup tapes and tape archives.

- Identify the personnel responsible for application support (*e.g.*, e-mail system administrators and others creating and supporting applications for specific departments or groups within the corporation).

The complexity of electronic information systems means that one needs to creatively and diligently determine who may be a custodian of relevant information. Custodianship may go beyond the obvious witnesses and decision makers. Interviewing secretaries and administrative assistants to higher ranked executives and managers is a good policy. More senior personnel who often do not maintain their own calendars and task lists or create their own computer documents are not likely to know the manner in which their secretary or administrative assistant maintains this ESI. IT or IS staff will often be the only ones with knowledge of centralized data stores, disaster recovery backup system, and other "back office" functions.

Developing a working relationship with IT department management, and fostering an appreciation of litigation demands, is crucial. The diversion of resources to litigation support is a significant concern because the IT department's priorities are geared toward corporate service and satisfaction, and outside litigation counsel are not part of the corporate chain of command.

2. Inquiries for Employees Who May Possess Relevant Information

- Computer hardware used:
  - Desktop and/or laptop computers
  - Home computers used for business purposes
  - PDAs
- Applications used:
  - E-mail
  - Instant messaging and social messaging (*e.g.*, Twitter)

- Message attachments
- Internet e-mail
- Shared e-mail systems with service providers, etc.
- Voicemail
- Desktop/laptop applications
- Word processing
- Spreadsheets
- Presentations (*e.g.*, Microsoft PowerPoint)
- Office management (*e.g.*, Microsoft Outlook)
- Databases
- Server/mainframe
- Reporting (*i.e.*, applications that generate sales reports, quality assurance reports, etc.)
- Project Management (*e.g.*, Microsoft Project)
- Shareware
- Internet and intranet usage
- Web logs (a/k/a "blogs" or "weblogs")
- Computer file storage:
  - Retention of e-mail and use of e-mail files/folders on desktop/laptop hard drives or servers
  - Retention of draft and final documents (reports, memoranda, etc.) on desktop/laptop hard drives or servers, even if the documents are retained in hard copy form

- Retention of downloaded files received from employees or other sources
- Retention of office-management files (*e.g.*, calendars and task lists)
- Retention of files or documents by administrative assistants or secretaries
- Use of removable media (*e.g.*, CDs, DVDs, floppy disks, and flash drives)

3. Considerations for the IS Department Management

- Overviews of departmental organization
- Policies and procedures regarding business retention of data and applications
- Overviews of tape archives and policies and procedures for retaining archived data and applications
- Retrieval of archived data and applications
- Overviews of backup and disaster recovery policies and procedures
- Retention procedures pursuant to litigation holds and preservation orders
- Overviews of applications and databases, and identification of any applications portfolios
- Overviews of e-mail systems and history of e-mail systems, including any outdated or legacy systems that may still retain relevant data

- Overviews of hardware, including locations (*e.g.*, mainframes and servers)

- Overviews of personal computers, including numbers and locations (*e.g.*, work or home)

- Other supported hand-held devices that store data or files

4. Considerations for IS or Information Security Personnel

- Backup frequency

- Retention of backup tapes before permanently deleting original data

- Overviews of disaster recovery systems and identification of any map or portfolio of disaster recovery

- Overviews of tape archives and identification of archived historical data and applications

- Databases or indices to archived tapes

- Retrievability and capacity to load and read archived historical data and applications

- Retention periods for archived data and applications

- Use of password and encryption technologies

- Retention of archived data and applications for litigation purposes

5. Considerations for E-mail Systems Administrators

- Overviews of system structure (*e.g.*, number of servers, number of post offices and mailboxes)

- Overviews of system capabilities (*e.g.*, attachments or folders)

- Volume of traffic

- Maintenance and retention of message logs

- Retention period for unread and read messages

- Frequency of permanently deleting items

- Shared systems with service providers, suppliers or corporate family

- Policies regarding system use

- Retention for litigation purposes

B. INVESTIGATING DATABASES AND APPLICATIONS

Counsel, together with the client, should identify the databases and applications that may contain relevant information and then identify the current and, if possible, former applications administrators. Applications administrators may be assigned by department, and the administrators assigned to relevant departments also may need to be interviewed. With respect to databases, interviewers should be aware of so-called "relational databases"—*i.e.*, multiple databases maintained on a corporate-wide basis from which specific information is accessed and processed to prepare reports formatted for particular departments or business purposes. System users likely are aware of only the reports formatted for their business use or the limited number of data fields that they can search. Questions for applications administrators may include:

- Descriptions of pertinent applications

- Descriptions of report formats and report format capabilities

- Identification of databases and descriptions of data sources and data entry

- Descriptions of how data are edited (*e.g.*, do new data replace old data in a field and are historical data retained)

- Descriptions of how the applications are backed up

- Information on whether historical data are archived

- Descriptions of whether applications have been significantly modified during the relevant time period and, if so, whether (1) prior versions of the applications were retained, (2) they can be reinstalled, and (3) data or reports can be replicated or generated

C. INVESTIGATING THE HARDWARE ENVIRONMENT

The client's computer-hardware environment should be investigated to determine what devices are available to employees and where the devices are located. The IS department is likely the best source of information. The inquiry should include:

- Availability of desktop and laptop computers
- Use of networks with servers
- Use of mainframe computers
- Use of other, hand-held devices that store digital information
- Use of home-based or employee-owned personal computers and laptops that have remote access to the client's hardware and may store information or files
- Use of CDs or other digital media to store historical records
- Use of digital voice-mail systems that store messages for extended periods
- Possible retention of tape recordings (*e.g.*, video teleconferences)

The objective of the inquiry is to determine where and how pertinent records might be stored and located. For example, if certain categories of employees are entitled to have remote access to the client's system, home-based personal computers may contain pertinent and discoverable records that either have never been imported to the client's hardware or may not have been retained by the client. In light of the 2006 amendments to Rule 26(b)(2)(B) that address disclosure and discovery of information that is "not reasonably accessible" it is also important to assess the burdens and costs that may be involved in retrieving and producing ESI from hardware, especially older or retired (legacy) systems.

D. INVESTIGATING BACKUP SYSTEMS AND ARCHIVES

Inquiries should be made of the appropriate information services or data security personnel to determine:

- The frequency with which backup tapes of data and applications are made (*i.e.*, daily, weekly, monthly or at longer intervals)
- Schedules for recycling and overwriting retained backup tapes
- Locations of backup tapes (on-site or off-site)
- The existence of additional sets of data and application disaster recovery tapes
- The existence of archived historical data and related applications
- The types of data and applications archived
- Locations in which archived materials are kept (on-site or off-site)
- Any ability to load and run archived data and related applications

Outside counsel should be aware that corporate management and in-house counsel often are not fully aware of the backup and archived materials maintained by IS personnel. In many instances, the culture of IT departments is to retain historical information whenever possible in order to meet the potential demands of their clients—the users of the system—and such departments may be far more concerned about being unable to retrieve information than they are about storing too much of it that long ago became useless.

E. IDENTIFYING VARIOUS APPLICATIONS

The rapid expansion and use of e-mail has captured the attention of litigators and legal commentators because some users consider e-mail to be (1) less formal than other forms of business communication and (2) as transitory as a phone conversation. Consequently, they often exercise little discretion in creating e-mails. But e-mail is only one type of business application that the litigator must investigate. Other types of applications include, but are not limited to:

- Engineering and computer assisted design ("CAD") applications

- Product ingredient and formula databases and applications

- Manufacturing quality-assurance applications, data collection and data storage

- Financial records data generation, storage and related applications

- Supplier bidding and purchasing applications

- Product distribution and sales databases, and applications including payment and accounts receivable data

- Advertising, marketing and product promotion databases and applications

- Customer and consumer information databases and consumer contact and complaint databases and applications

- Accident and incident report databases and applications

- Product testing and research report generation databases and applications

- External and governmental relations databases and applications, including lobbying expenditures and political contributions

- Indices of stored files, records and other document collections such as research or business libraries

- Litigation-related databases and applications

- Corporate web sites that might include representations about products or services, product warnings, consumer "hotlines" or links to other corporate data sets

- Databases and applications shared with service providers and suppliers

- Document management systems such as iManage, PC Docs or DOCS Open

- Litigation support applications from prior or unrelated litigation

- Collaborative editing applications (*e.g.* Share-Point)

- Desktop and laptop applications including word processing, spreadsheet programs, database software, presentation software and office management software

- Corporate intranets that contain items such as online corporate directories, corporate news and announcements, corporate policies and procedures, and corporate published statements

- Digital voicemail systems

- Video teleconferencing systems with possible analog or digital storage

- Web logs (a/k/a "blogs" or "weblogs")

Even this list is incomplete, especially for clients who are sophisticated computer users. But if a client has made a substantial investment in hardware and has an IS department or outside service provider, the client likely has developed and implemented a computer application for virtually all regularly conducted business activities.

CHAPTER V

PRODUCTION ISSUES

A. RULE 34: FORM OF PRODUCTION

The 2006 Amendments made two important changes to Rule 34. The first change addresses the form in which information will be produced. The Rule now permits the requesting party to specify the form of the production—*e.g.*, paper, PDF, TIFF, or native. The responding party may object but must offer an alternative. If the parties do not specify a form, and the court does not order one, then the Rule sets forth a "default" form of production—namely, the form in which the records are ordinarily maintained or in a form that is reasonably useable. Only one form is permitted per category of data (*e.g.*, all e-mails must be produced in a single form), but the form can differ by category. The second innovation of Rule 34 is that the Rule now specifically states that a requesting party may ask for a sampling of documents, ESI, or other tangible things.

Notwithstanding the clarity of the 2006 Amendments to Rule 34, the form of production of electronic records is fertile ground for dispute, often resulting from the parties' failure to communicate adequately on this issue. This failure is generally

the result of (1) one or more parties' failure to
specify a form of production as allowed by Rule 34
or (2) one or more parties' lack of knowledge of the
technological complexities attendant to electronic
discovery. Both of these pitfalls can result in costly
and time-consuming motion practice and, potentially, a court order requiring duplicative productions
in multiple formats.

In *D'Onofrio v. SFX Sports Group, Inc.*, 247
F.R.D. 43 (D.D.C. 2008), plaintiff moved to compel
production of defendant's business plan in native
format including metadata. Defendant had already
produced a copy of the requested document in accordance with plaintiff's request, which specified
that records be produced "in such files, or in such a
manner as to preserve and identify the file from
which such documents were taken." The court held
that this instruction could be interpreted only to
refer to paper document production, and plaintiff
had not specified a "form or forms of production"
for the production of ESI, leaving defendant free to
choose a "reasonably useable" form of production.
As a result, the court held that defendant was not
required to produce the document again in an electronic native format.

Had plaintiff specified the form in which defendant should produce the business plan in its document request, as permitted by Rule 34, plaintiff
would likely have obtained the document in its
native format with metadata, which would have
enabled her to access and analyze the business plan
both substantively and contextually, on par with

her adversary. In denying plaintiff's motion to compel, the court noted that plaintiff failed to demonstrate that native production was necessary and warranted.

Similarly, in *Autotech Technologies Ltd. Partnership v. Automationdirect.com, Inc.*, 248 F.R.D. 556 (N.D. Ill. 2008), the court addressed a defendant's motion to compel production of documents in native format even though defendant never specified this format in its requests for production and plaintiff had already produced the same documents in hard copy. The court denied defendant's motion to compel, explaining that defendant "was the master of its production requests; it must be satisfied with what it asked for." In addition, the court stated that defendant failed to demonstrate that the hard copy production was not "reasonably usable" within the meaning of Rule 34(b).

In *Lawson v. Sun Microsystems, Inc.*, 2007 WL 2572170 (S.D. Ind. Sept. 4, 2007), the court gave a lenient interpretation of Rule 34. Plaintiff sent a letter to defendant requesting production of all ESI in native format yet failed to specify the requested form of production in the formal discovery requests plaintiff later served upon defendant. In response to plaintiff's formal discovery requests, defendant produced paper copies of the responsive documents. Plaintiff moved to compel production of the documents in native format. The court granted plaintiff's motion holding that although plaintiff's letter was not a formal request, it "should nonetheless have provided Defendant sufficient notice of the form desired by Plaintiff."

The form in which e-mails must be produced has also raised questions. Surely the preference should always be for electronic production, revealing the important information of when the e-mail was sent and from where. It is also now beyond dispute that e-mails must be produced together with their attachments. This issue was addressed in *PSEG Power New York, Inc. v. Alberici Constructors, Inc.*, 2007 WL 2687670 (N.D.N.Y. Sept. 7, 2007), where, due to a vendor software problem, plaintiff produced three thousand e-mails divorced from their attachments. Although all e-mails and attachments were produced, the requesting party was unable to determine which e-mails and attachments corresponded to one another. In considering defendant's motion to compel a reproduction of the e-mails "in a reasonably usable form," the court considered the following three factors: (1) the relevance of the requested information; (2) whether or not it was reasonably accessible; and (3) if reproduction would be unduly burdensome or costly. After considering these factors, the court ordered plaintiff to reproduce the e-mails together with their attachments. Specifically, the court noted that production of e-mails divorced from their attachments did not comply with Rule 34's requirement that electronic information be produced as it is kept in the usual course of business or in a reasonably usable format.

Sedona Principle 12 suggests that requesting parties consider the following factors in determining what form of production to specify:

   a. the forms most likely to provide the information needed to establish the relevant facts of the case;

   b. the need for metadata to organize and search the information produced;

   c. whether the information sought is reasonably accessible in the forms requested; and

   d. the requesting party's own ability to effectively manage and use the information in the forms requested.

With respect to the new language of Rule 34, the question that has plagued the courts is what is the meaning of a "reasonably usable form." In *3M Co. v. Kanbar*, 2007 WL 1725448 (N.D. Cal. June 14, 2007), defendant moved to compel plaintiff to "organize" the electronic information it produced in response to defendant's "especially broad" requests for production. In an attempt to address defendant's concerns, plaintiff disclosed the custodian of each electronic document in its production. Nonetheless, the court ordered plaintiff to reproduce the requested information in a "reasonably usable" electronic format and required both parties to meet and agree on what is "reasonably usable." Although the court ordered plaintiff to reproduce ESI, the court noted that the discovery dispute was, in part, of defendant's "own making" as a result of defendant's broad discovery requests.

In *MGP Ingredients, Inc. v. Mars, Inc.*, 2007 WL 3010343 (D. Kan. Oct. 15, 2007), the court addressed a slightly different issue regarding production. In *MGP*, defendant produced approximately 48,000 pages of documents and ESI as they were kept in the ordinary course of business. Plaintiff moved for an order directing defendant to specify by Bates range which documents and ESI corresponded to each of plaintiff's discovery requests. Defendant objected to plaintiff's motion, arguing that Rule 34 only requires that "a party who produces documents for inspection shall produce them as they are kept in the usual course of business *or* shall organize and label them to correspond with the categories in the request." The court agreed with defendant, and in denying plaintiff's motion, explained that

> [t]he Rule is phrased in the disjunctive, and the producing party may choose either of the two methods for producing the documents. If the producing party produces documents in the order in which they are kept in the usual course of business, the Rule imposes no duty to organize and label the documents, provide an index of the documents produced, or correlate the documents to the particular request to which they are responsive.

The *MGP* court did comment, however, that this dispute might have been avoided if the parties had discussed this issue during their Rule 26(f) conference.

B. SEARCH METHODS

1. Strengths and Weaknesses of Keyword Searching

Upon receipt of a Rule 34 document request, counsel and client are under a duty to make a reasonable search for all relevant, non-privileged documents and ESI within the scope of the particular request (assuming the request is well-framed). The task of finding all relevant documents and ESI is increasingly difficult because databases of all kinds are growing larger and because of the inherent complexities involved in conducting searches through multiple collections of ESI. This problem arises as a result of the large number of ESI applications, as well as the broad variety of sources where ESI may be stored (*e.g.*, servers, databases, PDAs, backup tapes). Even in the simplest case requiring a search of online e-mail, there is no guarantee that using keywords will always prove sufficient.

EXCERPT FROM *The Sedona Conference® Best Practice Commentary on the Use of Search and Information Retrieval Methods in E–Discovery* (2007), 8 Sedona Conf. J., *available at* http://www. thesedonaconference.org:

Issues with Keywords

Keyword searches work best when the legal inquiry is focused on finding particular docu-

ments and when the use of language is relatively predictable. For example, keyword searches
work well to find all documents that mention a
specific individual or date, regardless of context. However, although basic keyword searching techniques have been widely accepted both
by courts and parties as sufficient to define the
scope of their obligation to perform a search for
responsive documents, the experience of many
litigators is that simple keyword searching
alone is inadequate in at least some discovery
contexts. This is because simple keyword
searches end up being both over-and under-
inclusive in light of the inherent malleability
and ambiguity of spoken and written English
(as well as all other languages). Keyword
searches identify all documents containing a
specified term regardless of context, and so
they can possibly capture many documents irrelevant to the user's query. For example, the
term "strike" could be found in documents
relating to a labor union tactic, a military action, options trading, or baseball, to name just
a few (illustrating "polysemy," or *ambiguity* in
the use of language). The problem of the relative percentage of "false positive" hits or noise
in the data is potentially huge, amounting in
some cases to huge numbers of files which must
be searched to find responsive documents. On
the other hand, keyword searches have the
potential to miss documents that contain a
word that has the same meaning as the term

used in the query, but is not specified. For
example, a user making queries about labor
actions might miss an e-mail referring to a
"boycott" if that particular word was not included as a keyword, and a lawyer investigating
tax fraud via options trading might miss an e-
mail referring to "exercise price" if that term
was not specifically searched (illustrating "sy-
nonymy" or *variation* in the use of language).
And of course, if authors of records are invent-
ing words "on the fly," as they have done
through history, and now are doing with increasing frequency in electronic communications, such problems are compounded. Keyword
searches can also exclude common or inadvertently misspelled instances of the term (*e.g.*,
"Phillip" for "Philip," or "strik" for "strike")
or variations on "stems" of words (*e.g.* "striking"). So too, it is well known that even the
best of optical character recognition (OCR)
scanning processes introduce a certain rate of
random error into document texts, potentially
transforming would-be keywords into something else. Finally, using keywords alone results in a return set of potentially responsive
documents that are not weighted and ranked
based upon their potential importance or relevance. In other words, each document is considered to have an equal probability of being responsive upon further manual review.

More advanced keyword searches using "Boolean" operators and techniques borrowed from

"fuzzy logic" may increase the number of relevant documents and decrease the number of
irrelevant documents retrieved. These searches
attempt to emulate the way humans use language to describe concepts. In essence, however, they simply translate ordinary words and
phrases into a Boolean search argument. Thus,
a natural language search for "all birds that
live in Africa" is translated to something like
("bird" + liv* + Africa"). At the present time,
it would appear that the majority of automated
litigation support providers and software continue to rely on keyword searching. Such methods are limited by their dependence on match-
ing a specific, sometimes arbitrary choice of
language to describe the targeted topic of interest. The issue of whether there is room for
improvement in the rate of "recall" (as defined
in the next section) of relevant documents in a
given collection is something lawyers must consider when relying on simple and traditional
input of keywords alone.

Use of Alternative Search Tools and Methods

Lawyers are beginning to feel more comfortable
using alternative search tools to identify potentially relevant electronically stored information.
These more advanced text mining tools include
"conceptual search methods" which rely on semantic relations between words, and/or which
use "thesauri" to capture documents that
would be missed in keyword searching.

* * *

"Concept" search and retrieval technologies attempt to locate information that relates to a desired concept, without the presence of a particular word or phrase. The classic example is the concept search that will recognize that documents about Eskimos and igloos are related to Alaska, even if they do not specifically mention the word "Alaska."

* * *

Other automated tools rely on "taxonomies" and "ontologies" to help find documents conceptually related to the topic being searched, based on commercially available data or on specifically compiled information. This information is provided by attorneys or developed for the business function or specific industry (*e.g.*, the concept of "strike" in labor law *vs.* "strike" in options trading). These tools rely on the information that linguists collect from the lawyers and witnesses about the key factual issues in the case—the people, organization, and key concepts relating to the business as well as the idiosyncratic communications that might be lurking in documents, files, and e-mails. For example, a linguist would want to know how union organizers or company officials might communicate plans, any special code words used in the industry, the relationships of collective bargaining units, company management structure, and other issues and concepts. Another type of search tool relies on mathematical probabilities that a certain text is associated with a particular conceptual category. These types of machine learning tools, which include "clustering" and "latent semantic indexing," are arguably helpful in addressing cultural biases of taxonomies because they do not depend on linguistic analysis, but on mathematical probabilities. They can also help to find communications in code language and neologisms. For example, if the labor lawyer were searching for evidence that management was targeting neophytes in the union, she might miss the term "n00b" (a neologism for "newbie"). This technology, used in government intelligence, is particularly apt in helping lawyers find information when they do not know exactly what to look for. For example, when a lawyer is looking for evidence that key players conspired to violate the labor union laws, she will usually not know the "code words" or expressions the players may have used to disguise their communications.

* * *

A recent case is instructive in its discussion of the importance of proper search techniques. In *Victor Stanley, Inc. v. Creative Pipe, Inc.*, 250 F.R.D. 251 (D. Md. 2008), plaintiff sought an order from the court that 165 electronic documents produced by defendants were not entitled to any protection as privileged attorney-client communication or work product protected material, as claimed by defendant. The documents defendants produced were part of a larger production of approximately 9,000 documents in PDF format that were collected using a keyword search. The court found that defendants failed to exercise reasonable care in performing the search, conducting no sampling of quality assurance: "Rather, it appears from the information that they provided to the court that they simply turned over to the Plaintiff all the text-searchable ESI files that were identified by the keyword search . . . as non-privileged."

The *Victor Stanley* court held that the party that inadvertently produced privileged documents and now seeks their return has the burden of proving that its conduct in reviewing and producing documents was reasonable. Indeed, even after the passage of Rule 502 of the Federal Rules of Evidence in September 2008, a party seeking the return of privileged documents that it asserts it inadvertently produced is required to show it took "reasonable steps" to prevent disclosure. *See* Chapter VIII, *infra*. Defendants in *Victor Stanley* failed to carry their burden. The court stated:

> Defendants have failed to provide the court with information regarding: the keywords used; the rationale for their selection; the qualifications of M. Pappas and his attorneys to design an effective and reliable search and information retrieval method; whether the search was a simple keyword search, or a more sophisticated one, such as one employing Boolean proximity operators; or whether they analyzed the results of the search to assess its reliability, appropri-

ateness for the task, and the quality of its
implementation.

2. Should Expert Testimony Be Required to Explain How Search Protocols Were Constructed?

Must a party proffer expert testimony to explain
how the search protocols were constructed so that
the court can have a basis to determine whether the
search was reasonable? This very question was addressed in *United States v. O'Keefe*, 537 F. Supp. 2d
14 (D.D.C. 2008), where the court found that expert
testimony was required.

3. Can Search Protocols Be Negotiated?

EXCERPT FROM George L. Paul & Jason R.
Baron, *Information Inflation: Can the Legal System
Adapt?*, 13 Rich. J.L. & Tech. 10 (2007) (proposing
the following negotiation protocol):

Step 1: The parties meet and confer on the
nature of each other's computer hardware and
software applications. Proposals are exchanged
on the scope of search obligations, in terms of
databases and applications to be searched, what
active and possibly legacy media are to be made
subject to search, and any limitations on scope
keyed to particular individuals within an institution, particular time periods, or other ways to
limit the scope of the search obligation. Key-

words are proposed as a basis for conducting
searches, with attention paid to negotiating appropriate Boolean strings of terms, with a full
range of proximity operators, wildcard, trunca-
tion and stemming terms (to the extent any or
all such techniques can be utilized). Alternative
concept-based search methodologies are discussed, to the extent either party has experience in using and has found to be efficacious in
finding documents. A timetable is agreed upon
for conducting initial searches.

Step 2: In the interval between meet and confers, parties conduct searches in accordance
with the representations made at the initial
meet and confer. Based on sampling techniques
or other methods employed, estimates are gathered on the volume of data potentially to be
made subject to search in light of the wording
of opposing parties' search requests.

Step 3: Returning to the meet and confer
table, the parties describe how initial searches
were conducted and what are the preliminary
results. Based on a finding that either too few
or too many files were retrieved corresponding
to particular specific requests, search protocols
are adjusted accordingly for a second round of
searching. If some form of open discovery measures are agreed to, an exchange of actual documents found as the result of the initial searches
takes place at this juncture, so as to provide the
opposing party with the opportunity to essentially request "more like this" (or not). Even,

however, absent fully open discovery, more limited reporting is made of search results, in order to narrow or expand search requests as appropriate.

Step 4: The process continues in iterative fashion as agreed to by the parties, until a mutually agreed time, or a mutually agreed cap on numbers of responsive documents is reached.

C. USE OF TECHNOLOGY FOR SEARCH AND REVIEW

1. The Use of Selection Criteria and Filtering to Manage ESI

Organizations of all sizes maintain large volumes of ESI on both active processing systems and legacy data storage systems, such as backup tapes. For any given discovery matter, however, the percentage of these large, commingled data sets likely to be considered potentially relevant is small. The question, then, is how should an organization realistically, reasonably, and defensibly review these large accumulations of data in order to cull out the small fraction that may be responsive to the matter at hand.

Traditional models of discovery, such as printing documents to a paper or image format for review, quickly break down when applied to electronic data sets of substantial volume. Even apart from the data loss issues associated with the conversion of electronic files to paper or image formats, the associated costs alone are prohibitive.

If the model of manual review does not work, can party-developed selection criteria be used as an automated methodology for identifying, locating, and retrieving potentially relevant data? Selection criteria are a form of filtering. The result of performing a search using selection criteria is a subset of the original data containing matches ("hits") based on the criteria utilized. Selection criteria can include specific search terms, combinations of specific search terms with Boolean operators, date ranges, time ranges, file sizes, file types, identified data sets, and other distinctive features or characteristics that could be used to identify the potentially relevant data.

In *ClearOne Communications, Inc. v. Chiang*, 2008 WL 920336 (D. Utah Apr. 1, 2008), a software copyright infringement action, the court became involved in the details of creating an effective strategy for searching the data from defendants' computers which had been "mirror imaged" in anticipation of a later search. The parties agreed on many of the search terms. Plaintiff accepted the search terms proposed by defendants and added five terms of its own. The terms were divided into three categories: " 'Name' (searching for names of specific individuals); 'Tech' (searching for a particular technological reference); and 'License' terms (searching for terms relating to the licensing of certain source code)." The only remaining issue presented to the court was whether the terms should be searched for together ("conjunctive") or separately ("disjunctive"). The court held that "Name" and "Tech" terms should be searched for conjunctively so the results would not be overly inclusive, producing a large amount of irrelevant information that would have to be reviewed. The court further held that "License" terms should be searched for disjunctively because combining these terms with others would be unduly narrow and may cause relevant information to be overlooked. The court also approved plaintiff's request to add certain limited search terms. The interesting point about this case is how involved the court became in structuring the initial steps of the search of the data stored on defendants' computers.

a. Typical Positions Taken by Those Seeking ESI

• Selection criteria cannot be comprehensive enough to ensure that all potentially relevant data will be identified.

• Search technologies are not reliable enough to ensure that all relevant data will be found.

• If selection criteria are chosen solely by the owner of the ESI, they are going to be biased towards not finding relevant information.

• We should be allowed access to all of the ESI in order to run our own selection criteria against it.

b. Typical Positions Taken by Those Holding ESI

• The use of selection criteria is an accepted and widely used methodology for identifying and culling potentially responsive information from the vast amount of electronic data that exists with various formats and processing platforms.

• We have taken steps to ensure that the selection criteria used are valid and reliable.

• Search technology does allow the use of selection criteria to be a reliable and effective means of finding data.

• We have the right to control our own data and to shield non-relevant, trade secret, privileged and other materials from the opposing party.

c. A Neutral Approach

In many cases, electronic data are found in broadly categorized groupings, such as in vaguely named sub-directories on an individual's hard drive, or in generic, commingled folders, such as an e-mail system's "inbox" or "outbox," or are otherwise not stored in a manner that can be used to efficiently identify potentially responsive information from the storage matrix alone.

A typical project involving large volumes of data would generally incorporate selection criteria and the searching of data as follows:

1.   Collect data from the client.

2. Sample or otherwise analyze the data set to determine the proper scope of data to be processed while keeping in mind the likelihood of discovering responsive data and the corresponding cost and time burdens.

3. Load the data into an electronic review platform for analysis.

4. Establish and validate appropriate selection criteria.

5. Filter the data using the validated selection criteria.

6. Apply annotation criteria to the data.

7. Perform review of the selected, annotated data in electronic form with appropriate responsiveness, privilege, and production determinations.

d.   A Defensible Selection Process

The steps required to develop and implement an appropriate data selection process should include the following:

i.   Analyzing Proposed Search Terms and Selection Criteria

The use of search terms either provided by a party or created by its consultant and various data parameters (*e.g.* date range, locations, divisions) determines the scope of the search. This analysis includes an assessment of the selected search terms and data parameters.

ii. Creating Search Criteria Using Standardized Syntax

The search terms and data parameters are then translated into a standardized syntax for expressing these criteria. This syntax combines simple structured English with notations taken from the discipline of formal linguistic analysis and specification in addition to appropriate operators utilized by common search tools. The proposed criteria are transformed into this format in order to implement the review of the data set.

iii. Validating Proposed Search Criteria with Party and Counsel

The standardized criteria are then reviewed with the party and its counsel to ensure that they are complete and correct. Changes are made if necessary.

iv. Testing Revised Criteria Against Sample Data

The final criteria are then tested against the data set. This testing involves searches using the final criteria and examining the results of the searches to determine if certain of those criteria are either over- or under-inclusive (*i.e.*, returning data that are not potentially relevant or missing data that are potentially relevant). Both "hit" and "non-hit" data are also analyzed using word-frequency and other statistical tests in an attempt to identify additional selection criteria.

Both the party and its counsel should participate in this examination to ensure that the results are appropriate. The results of this review may be used to further improve the selection criteria so that they better identify and filter potentially relevant data.

This test, review, and revision cycle may be repeated as many times as necessary to ensure that the final search criteria chosen are as accurate as possible. This process may also be repeated later if additional data sets are introduced that differ from the earlier sets.

v.   Finalizing Criteria into Appropriate Format for Expected Volumes

The finalized search criteria are then converted to the formats needed for use with electronic search tools. Different tools may be used depending upon the type of data to be searched, the need for online reviews, and the volume of data to be searched.

e.   Other Issues to Consider

The producing party may consider meeting with the requesting party to reach an agreement regarding the selection criteria to be used in later searches of the electronic data set. While this is not always possible or advantageous, there are situations when this type of dialogue can eliminate needless bottle necks (such as disputes over search terms), and validate agreed upon search criteria and processes.

2.   The Use of Technology for Review

The volume of ESI within the business world requires the use of new processes and procedures for effective review during discovery. Traditional models of document review do not allow for the effective and economic review of large volumes of ESI. This point was highlighted in *Treppel v. Biovail Corp.*, 233 F.R.D. 363 (S.D.N.Y. 2006), where the court addressed the benefits of using electronic search tools to conduct a proper search of ESI. In *Treppel*, plaintiff had rejected defendant's proposal that the parties agree on which electronic files would be searched and what search terms would be utilized. The court criticized plaintiff's refusal to negotiate a search methodology as a missed opportunity and noted that using search terms to conduct an efficient search would be an excellent way to begin a search of voluminous electronic records.

When electronic data are collected for litigation, the mailboxes of key employees and file storage areas are often copied in their entirety, thereby containing a mix of documents that may or may not be related to the matter at hand. Electronic document sets therefore require a more robust review methodology that can identify relevant and privileged items quickly and economically.

Document review tools that search and display electronic documents in electronic form offer many benefits that are not possible in a traditional paper environment. Paper records must be reviewed sequentially. By contrast, a review of ESI using electronic search tools uses any number of fields to find similar documents, revises the search as often as required, and then annotates similar items in bulk, thereby dramatically speeding up the review process.

A comprehensive electronic document review platform will provide features such as:

- Extensive pre-review analysis that identifies attributes about the data set, including type, file size, file quantity, date and time, ownership, or any other metadata associated with both the data set and the individual file.

- Group annotation capability that allows individual files to be labeled with an identifying annotation that can then be used to include, exclude, route, or otherwise manage the file during the review process.

- Data-type specific search capabilities that provide accurate retrieval of data based on both structured and ad-hoc keywords and other criteria.

- Scalability that accommodates virtually any volume of data without significantly affecting deadlines.

- Ability to integrate remote reviewers over the Internet or other network environment in a secure manner.

- A user interface that has been designed and tested for quick, convenient review.

- Centralized hosting of data files to allow effective security and data management while providing a central hub for reviewer access.

- Distributed hosting of files that will not function in a central hosted environment, such as extremely large files or files that require specific hardware or software to function.

- Seamless integration of traditional paper review processes, scanned images, optical character recognition files, and coded data sets.

- A multiple-litigation model that allows data to be loaded once and then used for many matters simultaneously.

- Remote diagnostics, update, maintenance, and support capability.

- Real-time modeling and work-flow management tools that allow for the effective management and oversight of simultaneous review by large, geographically dispersed teams in a controlled manner.

- Structured and ad-hoc reporting and analysis of data characteristics.

- Flexible production options, including automated production to paper or TIFF.

- PDF, HTML, and native format export to traditional litigation support programs, virtual reading rooms, and other online repositories.

- Structured review of "non-hit" data in order to validate inclusion strategies.

- Ability to allocate data to reviewers by theme— such as content, custodian, or hit score—to optimize review efficiency.

- Host and review in native form to greatly reduce cost.

- The ability to create a privilege log automatically using items that have been marked with a privileged designation, including author, recipient, date, and subject line.

D. METADATA

A large amount of ESI, unlike paper, is associated with or contains information that is not readily viewable on the screen. This additional information, known as metadata, includes information about the file that the computer records to assist in storing and retrieving the file. The information may also be useful for system administration as it reflects data regarding the generation, handling, transfer, and storage of the document or file within the computer system. Many forms of metadata are neither created by nor normally accessible to the computer user.

There are many examples of metadata including file designation, create and edit dates, authorship, comments, and edit history. Indeed, electronic files may contain hundreds or even thousands of pieces of such information. For instance, e-mail has its own metadata elements that include (among about

1,200 or more properties) the dates that mail was sent, received, replied to, or forwarded; blind carbon copy information; and sender address book information. Typical word processing files include not only prior changes but also hidden formatting codes that determine paragraph, text, and line attributes. The ability to recall, or "undo," inadvertently deleted information is another familiar function, as is tracking creation and modification dates.

Similarly, electronically-created spreadsheets may contain formulas, calculations, or hidden columns that are only viewable in the "native" application— that is, the software application used to create or record the information. Internet documents also contain hidden data that allow for the transmission of information between an Internet user's computer and the server on which the Internet document is located. So-called "meta-tags" allow search engines to locate web sites responsive to specified search criteria. "Cookies" are text files placed on a computer (sometimes without user knowledge) that can, among other things, track usage and transmit information back to the cookie's originator.

Generally, the metadata associated with files used by most people today (such as Microsoft Office documents) are known as "application metadata." These metadata are embedded in the file they describe and move with the file when they are moved or copied. On the other hand, "system metadata" are not embedded within the file they describe but are stored externally. System metadata are used by the computer's file system to track file locations and store information about each file's name, size, creation, modification, and usage.

Understanding when metadata are relevant and subject to preservation and production represents one of the biggest challenges in electronic discovery. Sometimes metadata are needed to authenticate a disputed document or to establish facts material to a dispute, such as when a file was accessed in a suit involving theft of trade secrets. In most cases, however, the metadata will have no material evidentiary value—it does not matter when a document was printed, who typed the revisions, or what edits were made before the document was circulated. There is also the real danger that information recorded by the computer as application metadata may be inaccurate. For example, when an employee uses a word processing program to create a memorandum using a template created by another employee, the metadata for the new memorandum may incorrectly identify the template creator as the author. However, properly used metadata may be able to provide substantial benefit by facilitating more efficient search and retrieval of ESI.

1.   Types of Metadata

When deciding what metadata may be relevant, consider these definitions from *The Sedona Conference Glossary of E-Discovery and Digital Information Management (Second Edition)* (December 2007).

* **Application Metadata:** Data created by the application specific to the ESI being addressed, embedded in the file and moved with the file when copied; copying may alter application metadata.

* **Document Metadata:** Properties about the file stored in the file, as opposed to document content. Often this data is not immediately viewable in the software application used to create/edit the document but often can be accessed via a "Properties" view. Examples include document author and company, and create and revision dates. Contrast with File System Metadata and E-mail Metadata.

* **E-mail Metadata:** Data stored in the e-mail about the e-mail. Often this data is not even viewable in the e-mail client application used to create the e-mail, e.g., blind copy addressees, received date. The amount of e-mail metadata available for a particular e-mail varies greatly depending on the e-mail system. Contrast with File System Metadata and Document Metadata.

* **Embedded Metadata:** Generally hidden, but an integral part of ESI, such as "track changes" or "comments" in a word processing file or "notes" in a presentation file. While some metadata are routinely extracted during processing and conversion for e-discovery, embedded data may not be. Therefore, it may only be available in the original, native file. *See also* Application Metadata and Metadata.

* **File System Metadata:** Metadata generated by the system to track the demographics (name, size, location, usage, etc.) of the ESI and, not embedded within, but stored externally from the ESI.

* **Metadata:** Data typically stored electronically that describes characteristics of ESI, found in different places in different forms. Can be supplied by applications, users or the file system. Metadata can describe how, when and by whom ESI was collected, created, accessed, modified and how it is formatted. Can be altered intentionally or inadvertently. Certain metadata can be extracted when native files are processed for litigation. Some metadata, such as file dates and sizes, can easily be seen by users; other metadata can be hidden or embedded and unavailable to computer users who are not technically adept. Metadata are generally not reproduced in full form when a document is printed to paper or electronic image.

* **Native Format:** Electronic documents have an associated file structure defined by the original creating application. This file structure is referred to as the "native format" of the document. Because viewing or searching documents in the native format may require the original application (for example, viewing a Microsoft Word document may require the Microsoft

Word application), documents may be converted
to a neutral format as part of the record acquisition or archive process. "Static" formats (often called "imaged formats"), such as TIFF or
PDF, are designed to retain an image of the
document as it would look viewed in the original creating application but do not allow metadata to be viewed or the document information
to be manipulated. In the conversion to static
format, the metadata can be processed, preserved and electronically associated with the
static format file. However, with technology
advancements, tools and applications are becoming increasingly available to allow viewing
and searching of documents in their native
format, while still preserving all metadata.

* **User–Added Metadata:** Data, possibly
work product, created by a user while copying,
reviewing or working with a file, including an-
notations and subjective coding information.

* **Vendor–Added Metadata:** Data created
and maintained by the electronic discovery vendor as a result of processing the document.
While some vendor-added metadata has direct
value to customers, much of it is used for
process reporting, chain of custody and data
accountability.

2. The *Sedona Principles* and Metadata

Several excerpts from the 2007 revision of *The Sedona Principles* dealing with the issues surrounding metadata are set forth below.

a.   Form of Production and Metadata

In the process of preparing the new Rules governing ESI, the Advisory Committee rejected proposals to mandate any particular form of production and did not take a position on the need to produce metadata. Rule 26(f) instead emphasizes the need to discuss this topic early to attempt to reach agreement, and Rule 34(b) provides a process for resolving disputes, while providing two alternative forms of production in the event the parties do not reach agreement or a court order is not entered: the form or forms "in which it is ordinarily maintained" or "in a form or forms that are reasonably usable."

The phrase "ordinarily maintained" is not synonymous with "native format." It is common for electronic information to be migrated to a number of different applications and formats in the ordinary course of business, particularly if the information is archived for long-term storage. Routine migration will likely result in the loss or alteration of some elements of metadata associated with the native application, and the addition of new elements.

Sedona Principle 12, in contrast, deals directly with the issue of the need to preserve and produce metadata. * * * *

Sedona Principle 12

12. Absent party agreement or court order specifying the form or forms of production, production should be made in the form or forms in which the information is ordinarily maintained or in a reasonably usable form, taking into account the need to produce reasonably accessible metadata that will enable the receiving party to have the same ability to access, search, and display the information as the producing party where appropriate or necessary in light of the nature of the information and the needs of the case.

Comment 12.a. Metadata

An electronic document or file usually includes not only the visible text but also hidden text, formatting codes, formulae, and other information associated with the file. These many types of ancillary information are often lumped together as "metadata," although some distinctions between different types of metadata should be recognized.

* * *

Aside from its potential relation to the facts of the case, metadata may also play a functional role in the usability of electronically stored information. For example, system metadata may allow for the quick and efficient sorting of a multitude of files by virtue of the dates or other information captured in metadata. In addition, application metadata may be critical to allow the functioning of routines within the file, such as cell formulae in spreadsheets.

* * *

The extent to which metadata should be preserved and produced in a particular case will depend on the needs of the case. Parties and counsel should consider: (a) what metadata are ordinarily maintained; (b) the potential relevance of the metadata to the dispute (e.g., is the metadata needed to prove a claim or defense, such as the transmittal of an incriminating statement); and (c) the importance of reasonably accessible metadata to facilitating the parties' review, production, and use of the information. In assessing preservation, it should be noted that the failure to preserve and produce metadata may deprive the producing party of the opportunity later to contest the authenticity of the document if the metadata are material to that determination. Organizations should evaluate the potential benefits of retaining native files and metadata (whether or not it is produced) to ensure that documents are authentic and to preclude the fraudulent creation of evidence.

Comment 12.b. Formats used for collection and production: "ordinarily maintained" v. "reasonably usable"

* * *

[T]here should be two primary considerations in choosing the form of production: (1) the need for, or probative value of both apparent and [hidden] metadata; and (2) the extent to which the production of metadata will enhance the functional utility of the electronic information produced and allow the parties to conduct a more cost-effective and efficient review. These considerations should be weighed against the negative aspects associated with each format. For example, production in a "native" format entails both advantages and disadvantages. Native production, which generally includes the entire file and associated metadata, may afford the requesting party access to the same information and functionality available to the producing party and, from a technical perspective, usually requires minimal processing before production. However, information produced natively may be difficult or impossible to redact or Bates number, and files in their native forms must be viewed using applications capable of opening and presenting the information without alteration. Suitable applications are not always accessible to requesting parties, who may also lack the equipment or expertise required to use such applications.

A native file production that includes a substantial volume and variety of file types could become very expensive and burdensome for the requesting party. In addition, since certain metadata could contain or reveal privileged, secret, or other sensitive information, an organization may determine that it must review such metadata before producing it, which can substantially impact the speed of production.

* * *

The routine preservation of metadata pending agreements or decisions on the ultimate form of production may be beneficial in a number of ways. Preservation of metadata may provide better protection against inadvertent or deliberate modification of evidence by others and the systematic removal or deletion of certain metadata may involve significant additional costs that are not justified by any tangible benefit. Moreover, the failure to preserve and produce metadata may deprive the producing party of the opportunity later to contest the authenticity of the document if the metadata would be material to that determination.

* * *

In determining the appropriate forms of production in a case, requesting parties and counsel should consider: (a) the forms most likely to provide the information needed to establish the relevant facts of the case; (b) the need for metadata to organize and search the information produced; (c) whether the information sought is reasonably accessible in the forms requested; and (d) the requesting party's own ability to effectively manage and use the information in the forms requested.

Producing parties and counsel should consider: (a) the relative risks of inadvertent production of confidential, privileged, and work product information associated with different forms of production; (b) difficulties in redaction, tracking, and use of native files; (c) whether alternative (e.g., "nonnative") forms of production provide sufficient usability (e.g., by providing adequate accompanying information through load files) such that the producing and requesting parties have the same access to functionality; and (d) the relative costs and burdens with respect to the proposed forms of production, including the costs of reproduction review, processing, and production.

* * *

In *Williams v. Sprint/United Management Co.*, 230 F.R.D. 640 (D. Kan. 2005), the court addressed the difficult issue of when a party is required to produce metadata when it produces records to its adversary. This case involved a plaintiff who claimed she was terminated because of her age. She complained that defendant had produced certain Excel spreadsheets relating to a reduction-in-force without its accompanying metadata, which the company had "scrubbed" from the spreadsheet without the agreement of plaintiff or the approval of the court. Plaintiff argued that these records should have been produced in the manner in which they were "ordinarily maintained" or "kept in the ordinary course of business." Defendant, in turn, argued that the production of these metadata would allow plaintiff to obtain information that was not relevant to the instant claims and that might be privileged. Defendant also pointed out that plaintiff had not specifically requested these metadata.

In ordering production of the metadata related to the Excel spreadsheet, the court used "viewability" as the determining factor in whether something should be presumptively treated as part of a document. Thus, the court concluded that all metadata ordinarily visible to the user of the Excel spreadsheet are generally discoverable. While the court acknowledged that there may well be a presumption against the production of other metadata, this presumption is rebutted whenever a producing party is aware "or should be reasonably aware" that particular metadata are relevant to the dispute. The court concluded that when a party is ordered to produce records as they are maintained in the ordinary course of business, the party must produce the records with the metadata unless it objects or the parties agree that the metadata need not be produced. Thus the court held that the producing party has the burden to object to the production of metadata because it is in the best position to determine whether there is a basis to object and because the metadata are a part of the record and removing it requires an affirmative act.

In *Wyeth v. Impax Laboratories, Inc.*, 248 F.R.D. 169 (D. Del. 2006), the court addressed a similar issue. Impax asked the court to order Wyeth to produce electronic documents in their native format with all the metadata rather than the TIFF image format in which they were produced. Wyeth, in turn, opposed this request arguing that Impax had not shown a "particularized need" for the metadata and collecting such data would be overly burdensome. The court held in Wyeth's favor finding that the parties had not agreed on a particular form of production and that Impax had not demonstrated a particularized need for the metadata. Finally, Impax did not argue (or establish) that there was a foreseeable need for the metadata.

In *Aguilar v. Immigration & Customs Enforcement Division of the United States Department of Homeland Security*, 255 F.R.D. 350 (S.D.N.Y. 2008), plaintiffs requested that defendants produce relevant documents in native format after defendants had already produced those documents without metadata. In considering plaintiffs' request, the court first analyzed the legal community's changing attitude toward metadata. In particular, the court noted that the Sedona Conference had initially expressed a presumption against the production of metadata but now favors the production of metadata when it is reasonably accessible and "enables the receiving party to have the same ability to access, search and display . . . information as the producing party." Applying this new principle to the facts of this case, the court explained that if plaintiffs had initially requested metadata with respect to word processing documents and powerpoints it would have been ordered, but because plaintiffs' request was tardy, they now had to make an enhanced showing of need. The court held that if the metadata would not materially enhance plaintiffs' ability to search the documents, it would only order production if plaintiffs assumed all the costs of this production. Defendants agreed to produce the metadata associated with Excel Spreadsheets. Finally, with respect to database metadata, the court ordered that defendants demonstrate the database to plaintiffs using "dummy" data to allow plaintiffs' expert to identify important metadata.

In *Lake v. City of Phoenix*, 2009 WL 73256 (Ariz. Ct. App. Jan. 13, 2009), the court held that the metadata at issue not public records subject to a public-records request. The court reasoned that because the metadata were merely by-products of a police officer's record creation, they were not records that the law required him to make in the "pursuance of a duty." Therefore, the court denied plaintiff's request for these metadata in plaintiff's second request to produce.

E. ON-SITE INSPECTIONS—NEUTRAL EXPERTS, CONFIDENTIALITY PROTECTION, AND INSPECTION PROTOCOLS

On occasion, a court will require the mirror imaging (a forensic duplicate) of the hard drives of any computers that contain documents responsive to an opposing party's request for production. Litigants often request a court-ordered inspection of their adversary's computer hard drives where the parties cannot agree on a protocol or there is evidence that relevant ESI will be found on a computer hard drive that the adversary has failed to produce. Such court-ordered inspections are warranted where the ESI in question goes to the heart of the action.

The federal courts derive their authority to order such inspections from Rule 34(a), which allows parties to request that another party

> produce and permit the requesting party . . . to inspect, copy, test, or sample . . . any designated documents or electronically stored information—including writings, drawings, graphs, charts, photographs, sound recordings, images, and other data or data compilations—stored in any medium from which information can be obtained either directly or, if necessary, after translation by the responding party into reasonably usable form.

However, Rule 34(a) is not meant to create a routine right of direct access to the opponent's electronic information systems. Court-ordered inspections of computer hard drives usually require on-site access and can be intrusive and burdensome, causing significant inconvenience and interruption to the business operations of the responding party. Furthermore, a computer hard drive is likely to contain a significant quantity of non-relevant, privileged, and confidential information which raises significant privacy concerns.

Courts therefore must carefully craft inspection protocols that balance the need for discovery of relevant information against the risk of disclosing privileged material and the undue intrusiveness resulting from inspecting or testing such systems. The

details of these protocols may vary depending on
the unique facts and circumstances of each case, but
generally include the following: (1) a forensic expert
will obtain the images of the computer hard drives;
(2) the party whose hard drives were imaged will
maintain the images; (3) the producing party will
have the opportunity to remove any non-relevant or
privileged information; and (4) the producing party
will disclose to the requesting party responsive information found on the images with a log identifying any material removed based on a claim of privilege.

Ferron v. Search Cactus, LLC, 2008 WL 1902499
(S.D. Ohio Apr. 28, 2008), is a recent case applying
these principles. In *Ferron*, plaintiff, an attorney
practicing law from his home, alleged that unsolicited e-mails had been unlawfully distributed by defendants. During discovery, defendants requested
an on-site inspection of plaintiff's computers to
determine if the e-mails were indeed unsolicited or
whether he had solicited the e-mails in order to
create a cause of action. Following a discovery conference the court determined that plaintiff had not
taken reasonable steps to preserve relevant information, had not produced relevant information,
and that plaintiff's hard drives were the only available sources of relevant information. As a result,
the court permitted an inspection of plaintiff's computers by computer forensic experts and issued a
detailed protocol covering the conduct of the inspection in order to protect both privileged and
confidential communications. The protocol required

the following steps: (1) plaintiff's expert shall create mirror-images of plaintiff's hard drives and preserve them; (2) plaintiff's expert may then remove
confidential personal information and explain to
defendants' expert the protocol he used to remove
that information; (3) plaintiff must then permit
defendants' expert to inspect his hard drives; (4)
defendants' expert may then create a mirror image
of plaintiff's hard drives; (5) defendants' expert
must review his findings with plaintiff before making any information available to defendants; (6)
plaintiff may identify information that he deems is
irrelevant and create a privilege log for any allegedly privileged information—defendants' expert must
remove the designated information before producing the remainder to defendants; (7) defendants'
expert shall provide plaintiff with the protocol used
to remove the privileged information. Finally, the
court held that both experts would act as officers of
the court and that each party would bear the cost
of its own forensic expert.

1. Denying Requests for On-Site Inspec-
tions

Courts have been cautious in requiring the mirror
imaging of computers where the request is extremely broad in nature and the connection between the
computers and the claims in the lawsuit are vague
or unsubstantiated. Mere conjecture or suspicion
that an adversary has not produced discoverable
information is not enough. For example, in *Heden-*

burg v. Aramark American Food Services, 2007 WL 162716 (W.D. Wash. Jan. 17, 2007), an employment discrimination case, defendant sought a mirror image of plaintiff's home computer. Defendant contended that plaintiff's personal correspondence with unnamed third parties (in the form of e-mails or Internet postings) might reveal discrepancies in her testimony about the alleged discriminatory events and the impact of certain events on her emotional state. Defendant argued that access to a plaintiff's computer was common in employment cases and offered to have the hard drive mirror image sent to a special master in an effort to resolve the problem of disclosing privileged or other non-discoverable information. Plaintiff argued that she had already made a diligent search of her computer files. She objected to the discovery as a fishing expedition and refused to permit defendant access to her home computer's hard drive.

The court observed that such a search is sometimes permitted where the contents of the computer go to the heart of the case. Here, the court found that the central claims in the case were wholly unrelated to the contents of plaintiff's computer and that defendant was "hoping blindly to find something useful in its impeachment of the plaintiff." In denying defendant's motion, the court stated:

Defendant essentially seeks a search warrant to confirm that Plaintiff has not memorialized statements contrary to her testimony in this case. If the issue related instead to a lost paper diary, the court would not permit the Defendant to search the plaintiff's property to ensure that her search was complete.

Similarly, in *Williams v. Massachusetts Mutual Life Insurance Co.*, 226 F.R.D. 144 (D. Mass. 2005), a wrongful termination case, plaintiff sought the court's help in obtaining from defendants a particular e-mail he claimed to have seen and possessed at one point, but no longer possessed. He sought an order appointing a neutral computer forensics expert to conduct the search for the e-mail, and in the event the e-mail was discovered, to conduct an additional electronic investigation "to locate and retrieve all electronic communications related to his employment and termination that have not as yet been produced by defendants."

In denying the request, the court reasoned that plaintiff had presented no credible evidence that defendants were unwilling to produce computer-generated documents, whether now or in the future, or that they had withheld relevant information: "Before permitting such an intrusion into an opposing party's information system—particularly where, as here, that party has undertaken its own search and forensic analysis and has sworn to its accuracy—the inquiring party must present at least some reliable information that the opposing party's representations are misleading or substantively inaccurate."

Even where there is some evidence that data on an adversary's computer systems are responsive, courts may deny a request for inspection by imaging where the burden on the responding party is too great. In *Ponca Tribe of Indians of Oklahoma v. Continental Carbon, Co.*, 2006 WL 2927878 (W.D. Okla. Oct. 11, 2006), the court rejected plaintiffs' request that they be permitted to image or download all information stored in defendant's "data historian" program. Plaintiffs initially proposed imaging or mirroring the data historian as a means of easily obtaining the requested information. However, defendant objected and argued that such imaging would necessarily require approximately one hundred days to complete and that any such imaging would violate the licensing for the operating software used by defendant. Plaintiffs further suggested that the information be downloaded into a database using defendant's software. Defendant responded that it did not own the software modules, but that such software could be purchased for approximately $5,000 and would require another $5,000 in training and programming to make the modules useable. The court concluded that production of the data historian information was unduly burdensome and noted that plaintiffs had failed to demonstrate that their need for the information contained within the data historian outweighed the burden of producing it.

2. Granting Requests for On-Site Inspections

There are times, however, when a court permits an on-site inspection of an adversary's computer. In

Cenveo Corp. v. Slater, 2007 WL 442387 (E.D. Pa. Jan. 31, 2007), plaintiff sought to have its expert create a mirror image of defendants' hard drives, which would then be searched for responsive information. Cenveo alleged that defendants, its former employees, had used Cenveo's computers to steal its trade secrets, confidential information, and business opportunities. The court held that an on-site inspection and mirror imaging of the hard drives was warranted "[b]ecause of the close relationship between plaintiff's claims and defendants' computer equipment."

Similarly, in *Ameriwood Industries, Inc. v. Liberman*, 2006 WL 3825291 (E.D. Mo. Dec. 27, 2006), another trade secrets case, plaintiff alleged that defendants—its former employees—had used plaintiff's computers and confidential files to divert its business to defendants' new company. The court granted plaintiff's motion to allow an independent expert to obtain and search a mirror image of defendants' computer equipment. The court based its ruling on "the close relationship between plaintiff's claims and defendants' computer equipment, and [had] cause to question whether defendants have produced all responsive documents." The court found that deleted versions of e-mails, which were not produced, might exist on defendants' computers, along with other relevant data such as where certain files were sent and whether defendants accessed other confidential files.

When courts permit inspection, they usually order measures to protect confidentiality, such as having an independent computer forensics expert conduct the imaging. In addition, the producing party is generally allowed to review the information for privilege and responsiveness before producing it to the requesting party. In *Ameriwood*, for example, plaintiff's computer forensics expert was ordered to first provide responsive files retrieved from defendants' hard drives to defendants' counsel, who could review the records for privilege and responsiveness before sending them to plaintiff's counsel.

3. Is a "Neutral" Computer Forensics Expert Required?

In addition to facilitating disclosure of relevant evidence, a central purpose of a court-imposed inspection is to protect the responding party's privacy and privileges in the ESI being searched. To this end, courts often require that the designated expert be made an "officer of the court" or be subject to strict confidentiality agreements or protective orders.

A key issue is whether the appointed expert must be independent and neutral, or whether it is acceptable to use the forensic expert of one of the parties. While some protocols call for independent experts, often one of the litigant's experts will be appointed to the task in order to minimize costs and complexity.

For example, in *Calyon v. Mizuho Securities USA Inc.*, 2007 WL 1468889 (S.D.N.Y. May 18, 2007), plaintiff maintained that only its expert—as opposed to defendants' expert or an independent expert—would possess the requisite incentive to search exhaustively for evidence. Defendants argued that granting plaintiff's expert "unfettered access" to home computers and computer storage devices would impermissibly invade the privacy rights of defendants and their non-party family members who also used the computers. Defendants proposed that their own expert review the mirror images by using search terms provided by plaintiff, or that a search be performed by an independent expert, who would presumably be appointed by the court.

The court denied plaintiff's expert access to image and search defendants' home computers and also rejected the suggestion that an independent expert be appointed to perform the work, noting that

[the plaintiff] does not appear to dispute that the defendants' expert has the technological capability to perform this search. Moreover, the [defendants'] counsel and expert have stated that they are willing to work cooperatively with [plaintiff]'s counsel and expert on an on-going basis to develop and refine search techniques to ensure that all responsive information is identified. In the end, other than arguing that only its expert has the proper incentives to conduct an exhaustive search, [plaintiff] provides no specific basis for why it believes the [defendants'] expert would not thoroughly search the hard drive images. [Plaintiff]'s argument about proper incentives is simply too generalized a basis for granting it *carte blanche* access to the [defendants'] personal hard drives, access that [plaintiff] itself acknowledges as "extraordinary." Finally, ... the Court finds no need, at this time, to appoint [an independent expert], which would introduce yet another layer of expertise to a case where each side has already retained experts of their choice, and which would make the prosecution of this action more costly.

F. DISCOVERY FROM MOST KNOWLEDGEABLE PERSON

Depositions of the "person most knowledgeable" are nothing new. Rule 30(b)(6) has long provided the right to depose the individual in the best position to know certain information, whose testimony speaks for and is binding on a partnership, corporation, or other non-individual legal entity. In fact, there was no change to Rule 30(b)(6) in the 2006 Amendments. However, since the advent of electronic discovery, depositions noticed under Rule 30(b)(6), or its state law equivalent, have taken on additional importance in counsel's effort to understand the creation, identification, and retention of potentially relevant ESI.

Persons testifying as Rule 30(b)(6) witnesses "must testify about information known or reasonably available to the organization." A witness designated as the most knowledgeable person is not simply testifying about matters within his or her own personal knowledge. Rather, this individual is speaking on behalf of the corporation about matters to which the corporation has reasonable access. It is improper for a witness to deny knowledge of facts within the knowledge of the organization as a whole or reasonably knowable by the organization. This is to avoid the gamesmanship by officers or managing agents of a corporation who are deposed but each disclaims knowledge of facts that must be known by someone in the company. In a further effort to address this problem, many courts have held that a party cannot present evidence on a subject after its Rule 30(b)(6) witness claimed to have no knowledge about a subject that is properly described in the deposition notice. When served with a "person most knowledgeable" deposition notice, an organization or corporation must therefore designate a witness who either knows the information requested in the notice, or who can reasonably obtain that knowledge.

There is some debate over whether or not the subjects outlined in a Rule 30(b)(6) notice limit the scope of the examination. The majority rule is that in the absence of an agreement, depositions are only limited by the relevance and privilege bounds described by Rule 26(b). However, some courts have held that the requirement that a party noticing the Rule 30(b)(6) deposition "describe with reasonable particularity the matters on which examination is requested" limits the scope of the deposition to the contents of that notice.

The topics covered in a 30(b)(6) deposition must be relevant to the claims or defenses involved and not be redundant. According to the Rule and its many state equivalents, the topics must also be stated with "reasonable particularity." In order to avoid delay and objections to an overly broad deposition notice, the party requesting a 30(b)(6) deposition should carefully craft the notice to describe the topics of examination. Rather than broadly seeking information about the computer systems in general terms, the notice should specify what particular aspect of the corporate information systems (*e.g.*, e-mail message creation, storage, and deletion) are to be covered.

Companies and organizations should consider e-discovery issues when selecting a "person most knowledgeable" for Rule 30(b)(6) depositions pertaining to electronic preservation and production matters. If the witness does not understand the systems and architecture involved in the request, the result could be prolonged litigation, confusion, and disputes over the costs of finding the appropriate person. Depending on the subjects described in the deposition notice, many organizations routinely designate an IT professional or record retention manager as the appropriate witness for "person most knowledgeable" depositions.

The "person most knowledgeable" may be a person or entity outside the litigation entirely, such as a storage vendor or third-party contractor responsible for system backups or archiving of electronic records. In fact, an organization cannot refuse to designate a witness on the ground that the potential deponents are beyond the control or direction of the company.

In *Heartland Surgical Specialty Hospital, LLC v. Midwest Division, Inc.*, 2007 WL 1054279 (D. Kan. Apr. 9, 2007), defendant moved to compel plaintiff to provide a knowledgeable Rule 30(b)(6) witness on a number of topics because the witness produced by plaintiff was unable to answer questions relating to plaintiff's IT system or its response to prior discovery requests. The court held that a corporation had an "affirmative duty to produce a representative who can answer questions." The court ordered plaintiff to produce another Rule 30(b)(6) deposition to answer the outstanding questions but denied a sanction of attorney's fees because the original witness had been able to answer some of defendant's questions.

G. WHEN MUST NOT REASONABLY ACCESSIBLE DATA BE PRODUCED?

Rule 26(b)(2)(B) explicitly limits initial discovery of ESI to information from reasonably accessible sources. Nonetheless, the Rule establishes a procedure for the discovery of not reasonably accessible ESI.

(B) A party need not provide discovery of electronically stored information from sources that the party identifies as not reasonably accessible because of undue burden or cost. On motion to compel discovery or for a protective order, the party from whom discovery is sought must show that the information is not reasonably accessible because of undue burden or cost. If that showing is made, the court may nonetheless order discovery from such sources if the requesting party shows good cause, considering the limitations of Rule 26(b)(2)(C). The court may specify conditions for the discovery.

If a requesting party seeks ESI from a source identified as not reasonably accessible and the parties are unable to agree on discovery from such sources, the party may move to compel. This procedure is sometimes referred to as a two-tiered approach, where the parties first examine information that can be provided from fully accessible sources and then determine whether it is necessary to search less-accessible sources.

The new Rule requires the responding party to bear the burden of demonstrating that data are not reasonably accessible based on the costs and burdens of recovering the data, while the requesting party must show good cause once that showing has been made. This is a change from the general presumption of the discoverability of relevant information.

In *W.E. Aubuchon Co. v. BeneFirst, LLC*, 245 F.R.D. 38 (D. Mass. 2007), the court provided an excellent discussion of the concept of accessibility. Plaintiffs, the employer, sponsor and administrator of certain benefit plans governed by ERISA, sued defendant, the third-party administrator of these benefit plans. Defendant, which was now out of business, held thousands of claim-administration records as scanned images, which were indexed only by the name of the claim-examiner, rather than by the name of the claimant, the date of service, the provider of service, or the claimant's employer. Plaintiffs requested all records relevant to the administration of the employees' claims. The court found that the estimated cost ($80,000) and time (4,000 hours) to manually review the entire collection and to retrieve the responsive records made these records "not reasonably accessible" under Rule 26(b)(2)(B). The court then addressed whether plaintiffs had nonetheless demonstrated "good cause" to require the production of the requested records. After considering the proportionality factors set forth in Rule 26(b)(2)(C) and the seven factors set forth in the Advisory Committee Note to Rule 26(b)(2)(B), the court determined that plaintiffs had established good cause and that defendant must produce the requested records at its own expense.

1. Using Sampling to Determine Accessibility

In an age where virtually all data are technically accessible, a rational and defensible approach must be taken in discovery to determine what data are reasonably accessible under the undue burden test or the cost test. As discussed above, a party in litigation only needs to search for, and to produce data from, accessible sources of ESI.

Rule 26 gives no guidance as to how the determination of accessibility can be made using real data. A successful declaration that information is "not reasonably accessible" effectively removes that particular ESI from the discovery process (absent a showing of good cause). The value associated with such a wholesale removal of data from further discovery virtually guarantees that there will be an incentive to interpret difficulty of any kind as a sign of "non-accessibility."

Certain forms of ESI—such as backup tapes, legacy data and multi-table enterprise databases—are often quickly labeled as "not reasonably accessible" because of the inherent cost and difficulty associated with incorporating them into the discovery process. Because of the benefit of removing a set of ESI from discovery, battles will be waged over how accessible a particular set of ESI is from a technical point of view rather than based on whether or not responsive data are likely to be found and whether the benefit of retrieval outweighs the cost.

a.   Everything Is Accessible—For a Price

The determination of whether a particular source of ESI is accessible does not primarily depend upon the types of data (format) or the types of media on which it is stored (form). There are hardware and software tools that can restore virtually any kind of data—for a price. Thus the primary issue is whether it is *economically feasible*.

The fundamental question is

"Will the uniqueness and/or quality of responsive data that I get from any particular set of ESI justify the cost of the acquisition of that data?"

This critical question should be addressed at every meet-and-confer and court hearing on the issue of the accessibility of ESI.

b.   Marginal Utility

In terms of discovery, the marginal utility of ESI is the probative value from one additional unit of ESI relative to the cost necessary to identify, locate, retrieve, review, and produce that unit.

The arguments that a particular set of ESI is not reasonably accessible include:

1.   There are no responsive data on [the particular source of ESI]. If a particular source of ESI can be shown to have no responsive data, then any cost associated with identifying, locating, retrieving, or reviewing it would be too much. Because there is no requirement to produce non-responsive data, there should be no requirement to deal with them in discovery, regardless of the cost. There is a tendency today to argue that if data are easily accessible—such as live (online) data—then they should be searched as a matter of course. This is as faulty as arguing that another set of data is not reasonably accessible just because it is on a backup tape. Both should be subjected to the marginal utility test.

2.   There are responsive data on [the particular source of ESI], but the same data are available in another, more accessible, location. If it can be shown that the same data can be retrieved at a lower cost from other sources— from an online source rather than from a backup tape, for example—then the lower-cost source is preferable.

3.   There are some responsive data on [the particular source of ESI], but the cost to obtain them is not worth the value the responsive data would provide. This is the classic marginal utility argument. While there may be some data on the particular source of ESI that are arguably responsive, there is something about the data set—its volume, quality, or uniqueness— that makes retrieval unnecessary when compared with the cost to recover it. To be persuasive, this argument requires enough detail to justify the claims being made.

4.   We have no idea what is on [the particular source of ESI] but we do know that it will be difficult and expensive to deal with. This is the classic argument that is often used in an attempt to remove a set of ESI from the discovery process. It fails to comprehend the concept of accessibility, and attempts to capitalize on the "burden and cost" language of the Rule without giving any consideration to the "undue" component. Although a given source of ESI will be difficult and/or expensive to deal with, such a fact alone should not be enough to remove that ESI from consideration.

The problem with the first three arguments is that in order to make them successfully, counsel will need to have enough detailed information about the ESI in question so that she can choose which argument to make and then defend it. The problem with the final argument is that it is simply inadequate because the concept of reasonable accessibility requires a weighing of factors.

c.   Sampling

At first blush, the argument about ESI, marginal utility, and accessibility can appear circular. In order to make a legitimate argument about accessibility, counsel must obtain information about the data contained within the ESI. But if counsel has such information, how can she claim that the ESI is not reasonably accessible?

While some systemic arguments can be made (*e.g.*, the underlying data processing platform has no relation to the matter at hand or the data set is outside the time frame at issue), the most common way to prepare an "accessible/not reasonably accessible" argument for a particular set of ESI is to use sampling.

Sampling allows one to test the questioned ESI and to extract the information needed to develop a marginal utility argument in a cost-effective and timely manner. The basis of all sampling is that a subset of a population will reveal something about that population as a whole with some specified degree of certainty.

2. How Should Counsel Address Rule 26(b)(2)(B) "Good Cause" Issues?

The Advisory Committee Note to Rule 26(b)(2)(B) provides a roadmap of the considerations associated with good cause. Theodore C. Hirt offers additional practical guidance in *The Two-Tier Discovery Provision of Rule 26(b)(2)(B)—A Reasonable Measure for Controlling Electronic Discovery?*, 13 Rich. J.L. & Tech. 12, 20–21 (2007):

Counsel for both parties will need to inventory what information sources were actually searched from the first tier. A court will want specifics on the "quantity of information available from other and more easily accessed sources." Counsel for the requesting party will want to be conversant with what relevant information the first tier of discovery yielded. The quality of that information will have to be assessed as well to support the requesting party's position that other information sources must be searched.

The responding party can defend its position effectively if it has been careful and comprehensive in its previous responses to the first tier of discovery. Counsel will need to document how it has provided information from the reasonably accessible sources. The more comprehensive the showing, the more reasonable a counsel's position will be that second tier sources should not be searched. Counsel for the responding party also should determine what information sources no longer exist, what kind of information was stored on them, and whether that information has migrated to other systems. That will be important because the court will evaluate the failure to produce relevant information that seems likely to have existed but is no longer available on more easily accessed sources.

3.   Should Courts Weigh the "Marginal Utility" of Allowing Discovery of Information That Is Not Reasonably Accessible?

The court in *McPeek v. Ashcroft*, 202 F.R.D. 31 (D.D.C. 2001), described the use of the marginal utility test in considering whether to allow discovery of not reasonably accessible information. In assessing burden under Rule 26(c), the court reasoned that

> [a] fairer approach borrows, by analogy, from the economic principle of "marginal utility." The more likely it is that the backup tape contains information that is relevant to a claim or defense, the fairer it is that the government agency search at its own expense. The less

likely it is, the more unjust it would be to make the agency search at its own expense.

In *Oxford House, Inc. v. City of Topeka*, 2007 WL 1246200 (D. Kan. Apr. 27, 2007), the court applied the marginal utility test and held that although defendant could potentially access certain deleted e-mails sought by plaintiff from defendant's backup tapes, production of those e-mails would be unduly burdensome. The court observed that discovery should generally be allowed unless "the hardship is unreasonable in light of the benefits to be secured from the discovery." In this case, however, the likelihood of retrieving the e-mails was low because the backup tapes containing the e-mails had probably been overwritten, and the cost to retrieve the data and search for the relevant e-mails was high. On this basis the court denied plaintiff's motion to compel production.

4.   When Are Objections Waived Under the Two-Tier System?

What happens if after discovery and production is underway, the producing party determines that some of the requested ESI is not reasonably accessible? Has the producing party waived an objection by failing to object promptly and state in its initial written responses that the ESI is not reasonably accessible?

In *Cason–Merenda v. Detroit Medical Center*, 2008 WL 2714239 (E.D. Mich. July 7, 2008), in addressing defendant's post-production motion for cost-shifting, the court reasoned that defendant could have designated the requested information as "not reasonably accessible" and refused to complete production unless ordered to do so before incurring the costs to recover the data. The court found that defendant had failed to timely move for relief under Rule 26(b)(2)(B) and reasoned that

> [i]t offends common sense ... to read the rule in a way that requires (or permits) the producing party to suffer "undue burden or cost" *before* raising the issue with the court. Under such a reading, a court would be powerless to avoid unnecessary expense or to specify any meaningful "conditions" for the discovery other than cost sharing. Furthermore, the requesting party would be stripped of its implicit right to elect either to meet the conditions or forego the requested information. The Rule, if it is to be sensible and useful, must be read as a means of *avoiding* undue burden or cost, rather than simply distributing it.

5. Is a Requesting Party Entitled to Take Discovery to Test the Assertion that the Information It Seeks Is Not Reasonably Accessible?

The Advisory Committee Note to Rule 26(b)(2)(B) explains that the requesting party may need discovery to test the assertion that certain sources are not reasonably accessible. Such discovery, which may include depositions, inspection of data sources, and limited data sampling, can help refine search parameters and determine the benefits and burdens associated with a fuller search. Data sampling has been adopted by courts as a method to address accessibility issues and determine whether further discovery is appropriate. Thus, the requesting party may issue a more targeted Rule 34 request, seeking a sample of information from the sources at issue.

H. COST SHARING/COST SHIFTING

1. Accessible Data—Rule 26(b)(2)(B)

With advances in technology, written communications now take place at lightning speed. As electronic communications supplant both traditional paper correspondence and telephonic conferences, employees now find it more convenient to e-mail or text message someone sitting in the office next to them rather than pick up the phone or walk next door. This has resulted in the creation and storage of massive amounts of electronic data, much of which is of an informal or personal nature. The costs of processing such voluminous amounts of data to find the few nuggets that are relevant to a specific litigation, compounded by attorney review time, are staggering.

Litigants find themselves held hostage by their data, and the costs of electronic discovery may force them to settle, despite the merits of their case. As e-discovery becomes a prominent part of litigation, litigants are frequently asking courts to consider cost-shifting.

The decision in *Zubulake v. UBS Warburg LLC ("Zubulake I")*, 217 F.R.D. 309 (S.D.N.Y. 2003), helped set the stage for the adoption of the 2006 Amendments that addressed these concerns regarding electronic discovery. This case addressed whether the cost of producing electronic records in responding to a document request may be shifted to the requesting party. Generally, the producing party bears the cost of production of electronic evidence, as with any other kind of evidence. But under some circumstances the cost might be shifted in whole or in part to the requesting party.

In *Zubulake I,* the court first noted that Rule 26 permits discovery of evidence that is relevant to a claim or defense and possibly to the subject matter of the action if good cause is shown. Thus, electronic data are discoverable so long as they are relevant, regardless of the form in which they are stored. The court then noted that it may be appropriate to consider cost-shifting when the cost of discovery becomes an "undue burden or expense." Generally speaking, discovery of electronic data does not impose an undue burden or expense merely because the data are stored electronically. If the electronic information is "accessible," then it is entitled to the same presumption that applies to paper records— namely that the producing party pays. Even with respect to accessible information, however, a producing party is entitled to argue "undue burden" if that burden is based on something other than the mere fact that the records are stored electronically.

The presumption changes, however, when the ESI is "inaccessible"—the word used by the *Zubulake* court prior to the adoption of the 2006 Amendments. The court held that when information is inaccessible a court should always *consider* cost-shifting. The court defined accessible information to include (1) "online" data or data archived on current computer systems (such as hard drives), (2) "near line" data such as that stored on optical disks or magnetic tape that is stored in a robotic storage library from which records can be quickly retrieved, or (3) "off line" data which is stored or archived in media such as removable optical disks (*i.e.*, CDs or DVDs) or magnetic tape media such as Digital Linear Tape, which can be easily accessed using standard search engines because the data are retained in machine readable format. The court defined inaccessible information to include (1) "routine disaster recovery backup tape" systems that save information in compressed, sequential, and non-indexed format and (2) erased, fragmented, or damaged data, which are considered inaccessible, because, in order to retrieve the information, data must be restored through an expensive and time-consuming process.

Finally, the court adopted a test for analyzing whether cost-shifting is appropriate. The court utilized a seven-factor balancing test in descending order of importance:

1. The extent to which the request is specifically tailored to discover relevant information.

2. The availability of such information from other sources.

3. The total cost of production compared to the amount in controversy.

4. The total cost of production compared to the resources available to each party.

5. The relative ability of each party to control costs and its incentive to do so.

6. The importance of the issues at stake in the litigation.

7. The relative benefits to the parties of obtaining the information.

The court emphasized that because any cost-shifting analysis is very fact-intensive it is important to determine what data might be found on the inaccessible media. The court found that the best way to do this is by using sampling techniques and requiring the producing party to restore and produce responsive documents from a representative sample of the inaccessible media at its own cost.

The *Zubulake* approach of limiting or conditioning discovery only if it is unduly burdensome has since been embraced by the 2006 amendment to Rule 26, which provides that a party need not provide discovery of ESI that is not reasonably accessible, unless good cause is found. The Rule specifically leaves the door open to cost-sharing in appropriate circumstances.

While the 2006 Amendments to Rule 26(b)(2) explicitly apply to cost-shifting for data that are not reasonably accessible, do the amendments also apply to accessible data? Rule 26(b)(2)(B) only applies to data that are not reasonably accessible, but Rule 26(b)(2)(C) applies to all data. Nonetheless, some courts believe that a question remains as to whether cost-shifting is available for accessible data.

This question was addressed in *Peskoff v. Faber*, 244 F.R.D. 54 (D.D.C. 2007), where the court held that "cost-shifting does not even become a possibility unless there is first a showing of inaccessibility. Thus, it cannot be argued that a party should ever be relieved of its obligation to produce accessible data merely because it may take time and effort to find what is necessary." The court also noted, however, that "the search for data, even if accessible, must be justified under the relevancy standard of Rule 26(b)(1)." The better rule, articulated in *Grant v. Homier Distributing Co.*, 2007 WL 2446753 (N.D. Ind. Aug. 24, 2007), is that cost-shifting is available even for accessible data based on the proportionality factors set forth in Rule 26(b)(2)(C). *See also* 2006 Advisory Committee Note to 26(b)(2)(B) ("The limitations of Rule 26(b)(2)(C) apply to all discovery of electronically stored information."). In short, the court always has the option of conditioning discovery on the requesting party's payment of production costs.

2. Not Reasonably Accessible Data—Rule 26(b)(2)(B)

As discussed above, litigants have been seeking means to ameliorate the related costs and burdens of processing and producing copious amounts of electronic data, often by requesting cost shifting. Under the *Zubulake* decisions, the accessibility of the data sought was a major consideration in determining whether to shift costs. However, the mere fact that data are inaccessible does not require a court to shift costs to the requesting party. The court must also analyze the utility of the data and other circumstances, such as whether the data can be found in more accessible locations.

Ultimately the *Zubulake I*, court came to the conclusion that plaintiff should pay twenty-five percent of defendant's costs to restore information located solely on backup tapes. In *Zubulake v. UBS Warburg LLC ("Zubulake III")*, 216 F.R.D. 280 (S.D.N.Y. 2003), the court applied the factors set forth in *Zubulake I*, but shifted only search and retrieval costs—the costs associated with making inaccessible data accessible. But the court explicitly declined to shift the cost of attorney review time. However, restoration of data is only one step in the electronic discovery process that begins with data management and ends in the courtroom or hearings. As noted in *Zubulake III*, the costs to restore and search the backup tapes represented less than two-thirds of the total costs for the production of the backup tape data.

Often the most significant cost driver associated with e-discovery is the human review and analysis of the culled data. The Sedona Conference estimates that the cost to review one gigabyte of text on average is $25,000. Thus, the front end work to reduce the amount of data pays significant dividends in reducing reviewing costs.

3. The 2006 Amendment to Rule 26(b)(2)(B)

The 2006 Advisory Committee Note to Rule 26(b)(2)(B) provides that the decision as to whether a party must search sources that are not reasonably accessible depends on whether the burden can be justified under the circumstances of the case. A court may permit discovery of such sources on a showing of "good cause." The Advisory Committee then listed a number of factors that might be considered under the "good cause" test:

> Appropriate considerations may include: (1) the specificity of the discovery request; (2) the quantity of information available from other and more easily accessed sources; (3) the failure to produce relevant information that seems likely to have existed but is no longer available on a more easily accessed sources; (4) the likelihood of finding relevant, responsive information that cannot be obtained from other, more easily accessed sources; (5) predictions as to the importance and usefulness of the further information; (6) the importance of the issues at stake in the litigation; and (7) the parties' resources.

In *Quinby v. WestLB AG*, 245 F.R.D. 94 (S.D.N.Y. 2006), the Magistrate Judge considered a request for cost-shifting in an employment discrimination case. The court addressed a request to shift costs for data that had been moved to backup tapes pursuant to a company policy of moving active data to a backup media when an employee is no longer employed by the company. Such practices are called "data-downgrading," and some courts have frowned on this practice. *Quinby* determined that the cost of retrieving data for six departed employees would not be shifted to the requesting plaintiff if defendant was on reasonable notice at the time of the data transfer that the data would potentially be relevant to resolving Quinby's claims.

The court then applied the *Zubulake* seven-factor test. Ultimately the court determined that thirty percent of the cost should be shifted. Again, the court was not impressed with the marginal utility of the e-mails that were recovered from the backup tapes by using many broad search terms:

> Even though these e-mails may be relevant, and I appreciate that discrimination is frequently subtle and often proven by circumstantial evidence, I find that merely 71 pages of relevant documents from that period of time is quite low when compared to the volume of documents produced, particularly considering that much of the alleged wrongdoing took place in 2003.... In light of the low number of relevant e-mails, and in spite of the fact that the e-mails are only on backup tapes, the marginal utility test is low and leans in favor of cost shifting.

In short, the court determined that because the marginal relevance of the retrieved e-mails was low, a portion of the cost of retrieval should be shifted to the requesting party.

I. PRODUCTION FROM NON-PARTIES PURSUANT TO RULE 45

1. How Can ESI Be Obtained from Non-Parties?

ESI may be obtained from non-parties by service of a subpoena. Rule 45 contains a number of provisions similar to those found in Rules 26(b) and 34(b)(2).

2. Does a Non-Party Have an Obligation to Preserve Evidence Relevant to Other Litigation?

EXCERPT FROM *The Sedona Conference Commentary on Non–Party Production & Rule 45 Subpoenas 3* (2008):

Third parties may have obligations to preserve evidence relevant to others' litigation imposed by contract or other special relationship once they have notice of the existence of the dispute. Some courts place a burden on the party to have the non-party preserve the evidence. And at least one court has ruled that the issuance of a subpoena to a third party imposes a legal obligation on the third party to preserve information relevant to the subpoena including ESI, at least through the period of time it takes to comply with the subpoena and resolve any issues before the court.

Case law does not require a non-party to continue to preserve materials after [it has] taken reasonable measures to produce responsive information. In some circumstances, however, the receipt of a subpoena may serve to notify a non-party that it may become a party in the litigation or in a future litigation. In that case the non-party should take affirmative steps to preserve documents responsive to the subpoena and the potential broader scope of the proceeding. However, service of and compliance with a non-party subpoena is not, in and of itself, sufficient to serve as a notice of future litigation.

For a more detailed discussion of this question, see Chapter II, *supra*, at 38–42.

3. Is Some Information Protected From Disclosure by Federal Law?

A number of federal laws limit disclosure of information. The Health Insurance Portability and Accountability Act ("HIPAA") was enacted in 1996 to address various issues related to health insurance and medical care. One of the purposes of HIPAA is to provide uniform privacy protection for health care records. Title II of HIPAA provides extensive rules regarding the secure storage and exchange of electronic data transactions and requirements pro-

moting the confidentiality and privacy of individually identifiable health information.

The Federal Wiretap Act prohibits the unautho-
rized interception and disclosure of wire, oral, or
electronic communications. "Electronic communication" includes e-mail, voice mail, cellular telephone
calls, and satellite communications. Online communications are also covered by the Act. Federal courts
have consistently held that, in order to be intercepted, electronic communications must be acquired
when transmitted and that electronic communications are not intercepted within the meaning of the
Act if they are retrieved from storage.

The Electronic Communications Privacy Act
("ECPA") extensively amended the Federal Wiretap
Act. The ECPA prohibits the interception of wire,
oral, or electronic communications; the use of electronic means to intercept oral communications; or
to disclose or use any communications that were
illegally intercepted. ECPA restrictions regarding
disclosure of stored e-mail information apply facially only to public systems and e-mails stored within
such systems.

The Stored Communications and Transactional
Records Act ("SCTRA"), created as part of the
ECPA, prohibits access to certain electronic communications service facilities, as well as disclosure by
such services of information contained on those
facilities. It provides a private right action
against those who knowingly or intentionally violate the SCTRA. The Act is sometimes useful for

protecting the privacy of e-mail and other Internet communications when discovery is sought from a non-party provider.

The SCTRA also prohibits service providers from knowingly disclosing the contents of a communication to any person or entity while in electronic storage by that service. It also prohibits the service provider from knowingly disclosing to any governmental agency any record or other information pertaining to a subscriber of the service. Accordingly, most service providers will not disclose such information without a subpoena.

Finally, the Computer Fraud and Abuse Act makes it illegal to access a "protected" computer under certain circumstances, including when the accessed computers are operated by or on behalf of financial institutions. The Act also makes it a crime to intentionally access a computer without authorization or to exceed authorized access, if the information obtained is from any "protected computer" and the conduct involves an interstate or foreign communication. A "protected computer" is a computer (1) used exclusively by a financial institution, (2) used by or for a financial institution, and the conduct constituting the offense affects that use by or for the financial institution, or (3) used in interstate or foreign commerce or communication.

A couple of recent cases provide good examples of these principles. In *In re Subpoena Duces Tecum to AOL, LLC*, 550 F. Supp. 2d 606 (E.D. Va. 2008), defendant State Farm issued a subpoena to AOL to obtain the e-mail of non-party witnesses relating to the claimants in an action against State Farm, the claims handling process of the witnesses' employer, and certain forensic engineering reports. The District Judge, upholding the Magistrate Judge's ruling, held that the ECPA barred AOL from producing e-mails in response to this subpoena, and that the subpoena was overbroad and imposed an undue burden under Rule 45(c) because it did not limit the documents requested to the subject matter of the claims and it imposed an undue burden on the non-party witnesses. The court relied on Rule 45(c)(1) which states that "a party or attorney responsible for issuing and serving a subpoena must take reasonable steps to avoid imposing undue burden or expense on a person subject to the subpoena." The court noted that this subpoena requested *all* of the e-mails of one of the non-party witnesses which, by definition, included private information unrelated to the litigation.

In *Jessup-Morgan v. America Online, Inc.*, 20 F. Supp. 2d 1105 (E.D. Mich. 1998), a subscriber sued AOL, alleging a violation of the ECPA, invasion of privacy, and other claims arising out of the provider's disclosure of her identity pursuant to a subpoena. Plaintiff had posted messages inviting users to see sexual liaisons with her lover's wife. The court held that disclosure of the subscriber's identity did not violate the Act because the Act specifically authorizes the disclosure of subscriber information to private parties.

J. CROSS-BORDER PRODUCTION ISSUES

When documents are created and stored outside the United States, retention and production requirements often conflict with the data protection laws of foreign jurisdictions. In today's globalized economy, corporate documents are often located outside the United States. Thus, when an American court issues a discovery order seeking electronic data or files residing abroad, the parties and the court must consider a number of issues.

- Does the court have jurisdiction over the party who owns the records?

- Does the country in which the records reside have a blocking statute?

- Does the discovery involve personal data?

- Who controls the records?

- Is the personal data protected by a privacy law or other directive?

The interplay between Rule 34 document requests and foreign data privacy laws creates many problems. This is not surprising given the philosophical differences between the United States and many other countries with respect to the privacy of records. Our civil litigation system permits very broad discovery by private parties against private parties. The European system, by contrast, protects private records from disclosure and makes such records exceedingly difficult to obtain by private parties. The most acute problem concerns employee records.

In many cases, American discovery requirements squarely conflict with the 1995 European Union Data Protection Directive. Article I of the Data Protection Directive states that "each Member State shall protect the fundamental rights and freedoms of natural persons, and in particular their right to privacy with respect to the processing of personal data." Thus, the right to privacy covering personal data is deemed a fundamental human right. Many other countries also have EU-style data protection laws—including, for example, Argentina, Australia, Canada, Hong Kong, Japan, New Zealand, and Russia.

Beyond data privacy laws, many countries have enacted blocking statutes that either prohibit the disclosure, copying, inspection, or removal of documents from the country or protect the commercial interests of the country's citizens from cross-border interference from other countries. Most of these blocking statutes are civil; but in 1980, France made it a crime for private parties to conduct discovery in France for litigation abroad. Recently, the high court of France upheld the 2007 conviction of a French lawyer for violating the French blocking statute. The lawyer, who was assisting American counsel in *Strauss v. Credit Lyonnais*, discussed below, had sought a statement from an ex-director of Credit Lyonnais, without first obtaining consent or following the procedures of the Hague Convention. Switzerland has also criminalized the voluntary production of banking records, which protects the assets and records of depositors from the reach of foreign governments.

However, American courts have not deferred to foreign restrictions. In 1987, the Supreme Court held in *Société Nationale Industrielle Aérospatiale v. United States District Court for the Southern District of Iowa*, 482 U.S. 522 (1987), that the Hague Convention does not preempt the Federal Rules of Civil Procedure with respect to discovery. The Court further held that the Hague Convention provides neither exclusive nor mandatory procedures for obtaining documents and information located in a foreign signatory's territory. Rather, the plain language of the Convention, as well as its history, "supports the conclusion that it was intended to establish optional procedures that would facilitate the taking of evidence abroad." Accordingly, the Convention does not deprive district courts of their jurisdiction to order a non-American party to produce evidence physically located within a signatory nation. Any contrary holding, the Court reasoned, would "effectively subject every American court hearing a case involving a national of a contracting state to the internal laws of that state."

The Court noted three important reasons for its holding. *First*, a foreign party could obtain discovery under the Federal Rules of Civil Procedure, while a domestic party in the same suit would be required to resort first to the procedures of the Hague Convention. *Second*, unfair competition would result because if two companies were sued—

one foreign and one domestic—the foreign company would be subject to less extensive discovery procedures than the American company, even though the foreign company voluntarily chose to do business in the U.S. *Third,*

> since a rule of first use of the Hague Convention would apply to cases in which a foreign party is a national of a contracting state, but not to cases in which a foreign party is a national of any other foreign state, the rule would confer an unwarranted advantage on some [foreign companies over others].

The Court rejected the French manufacturer's appeal to principles of state sovereignty and international comity. In doing so the Court explained that

> the [blocking] statutes do not deprive an American court of the power to order a party subject to its jurisdiction to produce evidence even though the act of production may violate that statute. Nor can the enactment of such a statute by a foreign nation require American courts to engraft a rule of first resort onto the Hague Convention, or otherwise to provide the nationals of such a country with a preferred status in our courts.

In his dissenting opinion Justice Blackmun stated that

> I can only hope that courts faced with discovery requests for materials in foreign countries will avoid the parochial views that too often have

characterized the decisions to date. Many of the considerations that lead me to the conclusion that there should be a general presumption favoring use of the Convention should also carry force when courts analyze particular cases. The majority fails to offer guidance in this endeavor, and thus it has missed its opportunity to provide predictable and effective procedures for international litigants in United States courts.

Since 1987, Justice Blackmun's fear has been realized, as a number of American courts have ordered litigants to proceed with discovery even where foreign privacy limitations have been invoked. In *Hagenbuch v. 3B6 Sistemi Elettronici Industriali S.R.L.*, 2005 WL 6246195 (N.D. Ill. Sept. 12, 2005), the court ordered discovery from defendant's parent company in Italy, despite Italy's express declaration that it would refuse to execute any Letters of Request under the Hague Convention. The court found that Italy's sovereign interest in protecting its nationals from discovery was simply not compelling. In *Bodner v. Paribas*, 202 F.R.D. 370 (E.D.N.Y. 2000), the court found that neither the French defendants' privacy interests nor France's national interest in protecting privacy compelled the court to recognize the country's blocking statute. In *In re Vitamins Antitrust Litigation*, 2001 WL 1049433 (D.D.C. June 20, 2001), the court recognized foreign privacy interests by allowing foreign defendants to file a "privacy log" of documents protected from discovery by Swiss and

German law, but it otherwise proceeded with discovery under the Federal Rules. Finally, in *Reino de Espana v. American Bureau of Shipping*, 2006 WL 3208579 (S.D.N.Y. Nov. 3, 2006), a case brought by the nation of Spain in the U.S., the court found that the Federal Rules governed discovery and ordered Spain to search its officials' computers and e-mails for responsive information, despite Spanish privacy laws protecting such information.

Most recently, in *Strauss v. Credit Lyonnais, S.A.*, 242 F.R.D. 199 (E.D.N.Y. 2007), plaintiffs sought discovery of financial records related to support for Hamas, an alleged terrorist organization, that were held by Credit Lyonnais. Credit Lyonnais objected to plaintiffs' discovery requests on the ground that they sought disclosure of information protected by French secrecy laws. Credit Lyonnais argued that failure to comply with these regulations constituted a criminal offense that was punishable by imprisonment and fines.

In addressing whether Credit Lyonnais should produce the documents, the court considered seven factors set forth by the Supreme Court in *Aerospatiale* and now found at section 442(1)(c) of the Restatement of Foreign Relations Law of the United States:

1) the importance to the ... litigation of the documents or other information requested;

2) the degree of specificity of the request;

3) whether the information originated in the United States;

4) the availability of alternative means of securing the information;

5) the extent to which noncompliance with the request would undermine important interests of the United States, or compliance with the request would undermine the important interests of the state where the information is located;

6) the competing interests of the nations whose laws are in conflict; and

7) the hardship of compliance on the party or witness from whom discovery is sought.

The court found that the United States and France shared a "mutual interest" in "thwarting terrorist financing" and that this interest "outweigh[ed] the French interest in preserving bank customer secrecy"; that "the requested discovery originated outside of the United States, [was] crucial to the litigation, and [was] specifically tailored to the issues in this case"; that "plaintiffs [did] not have viable alternative means of securing the discovery"; and that Credit Lyonnais had "not demonstrated that it [was] likely to face substantial hardship by complying with plaintiffs' discovery requests." As a result, the court granted plaintiffs' discovery request.

In *Columbia Pictures, Inc. v. Bunnell*, 245 F.R.D. 443 (C.D. Cal. 2007), defendants had engaged a third-party web hosting service in the Netherlands a month prior to the Magistrate Judge's evidentiary hearing on the issue of whether RAM data had to be preserved and produced. Defendants argued that they could not provide the requested discovery because to do so would violate a Dutch blocking statute and thus subject them to civil and criminal penalties.

The court summed up what has become the federal consensus: "[foreign] statutes do not deprive an American court of the power to order a party subject to its jurisdiction to produce evidence even though the act of production may violate that statute." In short, the conflict between American discovery requirements and international data protection laws is stark and at the moment can be described as insurmountable. As a general matter, American courts are unwilling to ease discovery requirements in deference to foreign restrictions on document disclosure.

CHAPTER VI

SPOLIATION AND SANCTIONS

A. POWER OF THE COURT TO SANCTION

1. Rule 37 in General

Rule 37(a) of the Federal Rules of Civil Procedures gives the court power to issue orders to compel disclosure or discovery, and Rule 37(b) gives the court power to sanction a party for failure to comply with such an order. The court has broad discretion to determine the appropriate sanction. The following sanctions are identified in Rule 37(b)(2)(A):

(i) directing that the matters embraced in the order or other designated facts be taken as established for purposes of the action, as the prevailing party claims;

(ii) prohibiting the disobedient party from supporting or opposing designated claims or defenses, or from introducing designated matters in evidence;

(iii) striking pleadings in whole or in part;

(iv) staying further proceedings until the order is obeyed;

(v) dismissing the action or proceeding in whole or in part;

(vi) rendering a default judgment against the disobedient party; or

(vii) treating as contempt of court the failure to obey any order. . . .

At a minimum, Rule 37 provides that the court "must order the disobedient party, the attorney advising that party, or both to pay the reasonable expenses, including attorney's fees, caused by the failure, unless the failure was substantially justified or other circumstances make an award of expenses unjust."

In addition to the remedies available to the court under Rule 37, the court also has the power to sanction an attorney for violation of Rule 26(g), which requires an attorney to certify "to the best of the person's knowledge, information, and belief formed after a reasonable inquiry," the following: that disclosures are complete and correct, and that discovery requests, responses and objections are consistent with law, not interposed for any improper purpose, and neither unreasonable nor unduly burdensome or expensive. A sanction under this Rule may include an order to pay reasonable expenses, including attorney's fees.

2. Inherent Authority

Even in the absence of a discovery order under Rule 37 or a violation of Rule 26(g), a court may impose sanctions on a party for misconduct in discovery under its inherent power to manage its own affairs. In *Chambers v. NASCO, Inc.*, 501 U.S. 32 (1991), the Supreme Court held that "certain implied powers must necessarily result to our Courts of justice from the nature of their institution, powers which cannot be dispensed with in a Court, because they are necessary to the exercise of all others." The Court went on to say that "when there is bad-faith conduct in the course of litigation that could be adequately sanctioned under the Rules, the court ordinarily should rely on the Rules, rather than the inherent power. But if, in the informed discretion of the court, neither the statute nor the Rules are up to the task, the court may safely rely on its inherent power." Examples of sanctionable conduct not explicitly contemplated by the Rules may include obstreperous behavior during conferences, depositions, or document productions, or misrepresentations made in correspondence with opposing counsel or in court.

B. SPOLIATION

1. Definition and Elements

Broadly speaking, "spoliation" is the wrongful destruction of evidence. However, not all destruction of evidence constitutes spoliation, and even if spoliation is established, the range of potential remedies—from case management orders to sanctions—is quite broad.

Because of the volume and complexity of ESI that may be subject to discovery, there are vastly increased opportunities for parties and their lawyers to negligently or willfully alter or lose potentially discoverable ESI. The growth of electronic discovery has been accompanied by a growth in the volume and complexity of spoliation case law. Federal courts do not take a uniform approach to spoliation claims. In addition, Rule 37(e)[1] of the Federal Rules of Civil Procedure added an overlay to spoliation law that applies solely to electronic discovery.

Three elements are common to all considerations of spoliation. *First*, a duty to preserve the evidence must have attached before the evidence was destroyed or altered. *Second*, the party accused of destroying or altering the evidence must have acted with a "culpable state of mind." *Third,* the party charging spoliation must have been prejudiced by the act of destruction or alteration. When determining whether to impose sanctions and which sanctions are most appropriate, courts take into account the degree of culpability and the degree of prejudice to the innocent party. Other factors that the court may consider include: (1) the degree of interference with the judicial process; (2) whether a lesser sanction will remedy the harm; (3) whether sanctions are necessary to deter similar conduct; and (4)

1. In December 2007, the restyled Federal Rules of Civil Procedure took effect, resulting in the renumbering of Rule 37(f) as Rule 37(e). Therefore cases decided between December 2006 and December 2007 citing Fed. R. Civ. P. 37(f) are actually referring to current Fed. R. Civ. P. 37(e).

whether sanctions will unfairly punish an innocent party for spoliation committed by an attorney.

The first element, the duty of preservation, is discussed in Chapter II, *supra*. The second and third elements, culpability and prejudice—topics of significant dispute—are discussed below. Rule 37(e) restricts the power of the court to sanction parties under a narrow set of circumstances, but the range of sanctions for spoliation remains broad, as discussed at the end of this chapter.

a.   Degree of Culpability

Culpable conduct that may result in the loss or alteration of ESI falls along a sliding scale that includes mere negligence, gross negligence, recklessness, bad faith, and intentional misconduct. A sharp split of authority exists between the Eighth Circuit, which requires "a finding of intentional destruction indicating a desire to suppress the truth," and the Second Circuit, in which mere negligence will meet the culpability standard. Courts in other circuits line up on various points on the culpability spectrum.

i.   *Residential Funding*

In the first federal appeals court decision to discuss sanctions for the failure to produce ESI, the Second Circuit held in *Residential Funding Corp. v. DeGeorge Financial Corp.*, 306 F.3d 99 (2d Cir. 2002), that "discovery sanctions, including an adverse inference instruction, may be imposed where a party has breached a discovery obligation not only through bad faith or gross negligence, but also through ordinary negligence." *Residential Funding* was a breach of contract action in which defendant requested e-mail. Plaintiff did not object to the request, but responded that the relevant e-mail would need to be retrieved from disaster-recovery backup tapes, which would require it to seek technical assistance and more time to respond. Over the next several weeks, plaintiff repeatedly asked for extensions of time, and eventually produced only a few largely irrelevant e-mails. Plaintiff finally produced the raw tapes to defendant three days before trial, but refused to provide any technical information to assist in the restoration or retrieval of e-mail. Within four days defendant's technicians had restored 950,000 e-mails from the tapes and within a week had begun printing 4,000 e-mails deemed responsive. However, it was too late. The trial proceeded without the evidence. Defendant moved for the sanction of an adverse inference instruction, which the trial judge denied, finding that plaintiff had not acted in bad faith nor with gross negligence. The jury returned a large verdict for plaintiff. The appellate court reversed the decision, vacated the judgment and remanded to the trial court, holding that even the negligent destruction of evidence may warrant an adverse inference. However, the appellate court found that plaintiff's "purposeful sluggishness" in producing the e-mail suggested more than negligence. While the failure to properly handle the ESI may have been due to negligence, and did not result in the actual destruction of the ESI, the failure to adequately communicate with opposing counsel and the court, and the ultimate failure to remedy the situation and make the ESI available in a timely fashion, were "purposeful" according to the district court's findings.

Before *Residential Funding,* the Second Circuit recognized the need to treat the question of culpability on a case-by-case basis. In *Reilly v. Natwest Markets Group, Inc.,* 181 F.3d 253 (2d Cir. 1999), the court stated: "Our case-by-case approach to the failure to produce relevant evidence seems to be working. Such failures occur along the continuum of fault ranging from innocence through the degrees of negligence to intentionality.... [I]t makes little sense to confine promotion of [the remedial purpose of sanctions] to cases involving only outrageous culpability, where the party victimized by the spoliation is prejudiced irrespective of whether the spoliator acted with intent or gross negligence."

ii.   *Stevenson v. Union Pacific*

In contrast to the Second Circuit approach to culpability, which may include negligence, the Eighth Circuit announced a very different standard in *Stevenson v. Union Pacific Railroad Co.,* 354 F.3d 739 (8th Cir. 2004). The case arose from a fatal car-train grade crossing accident. Plaintiffs filed a motion for sanctions on the ground that Union Pacific had destroyed a voice tape of conversations between the train crew and dispatchers at the time of the accident and track maintenance records from before the accident. Union Pacific argued that sanctions were not justified because it destroyed the documents in good faith pursuant to its routine document retention policies. The district court imposed the sanction of an adverse inference instruction regarding the destroyed evidence and an award of costs and attorneys' fees incurred as a result of the spoliation.

On appeal, the Eighth Circuit upheld the trial court's decision in regard to the destruction of the voice recordings but reversed as to destruction of the track maintenance records. With respect to the voice tapes, the court found that defendant knew that the tapes would be important in any litigation involving the accident, that these tapes were the only contemporaneous recordings of conversations at the time of the accident and that defendant had preserved voice tapes in other cases where it thought the information would be favorable to it. This pointed to defendant's bad faith in destroying the voice tapes. By contrast, the court found that the pre-litigation destruction of the track maintenance records was part of a routine document destruction policy and that there was no evidence that defendant acted in bad faith in destroying these records well before the accident. The court concluded "there must be some indication of an intent to destroy the evidence for the purpose of obstructing or suppressing the truth in order to impose the sanction of an adverse inference instruction."

iii. The Circuit Court Culpability Line-Up

The degree of culpability on the part of the bad actor that is necessary to support a sanction of spoliation is still unsettled. There is clearly a circuit split on this question and decisions within circuits also reach differing results. This disarray may be explained, in part, by the differing facts of each case and by the severity of the sanctions that courts consider.

Broadly speaking, the Fifth, Seventh, and Tenth Circuits require a finding of "bad faith,"—which appears to be synonymous with intent—prior to imposing a sanction for spoliation, in accord with the Eighth Circuit decision in *Stevenson*.

Decisions from the Third, D.C. and Federal Circuits are in accord with the Second Circuit's view that negligence is sufficient to establish culpability for spoliation. Ninth Circuit decisions addressing dismissal as a sanction for spoliation have required a finding of willfulness, fault, or bad faith. However, at least one district court in that Circuit has expressly adopted the Second Circuit's rule that a finding of negligence satisfies the culpability factor in a spoliation analysis.

The Fourth and Sixth Circuits have adopted a "willfulness" standard, which falls somewhere along the spectrum between negligence and bad faith. Yet, in both of those circuits at least one district court has held that a finding of negligent conduct can support a sanction for spoliation. In the Eleventh Circuit, one district court denied an adverse inference sanction because there was no proof that the alleged spoliator had acted in bad faith, but another district court held that spoliation resulting from negligent conduct could support a sanction.

Perhaps the most distinctive approach to culpability is that of the First Circuit, which leaves the question of a spoliation finding to the fact finder with no required finding of any particular degree of culpability. In *Testa v. Wal-Mart Stores, Inc.*, 144 F.3d 173 (1st Cir. 1998), the court held that the proponent of an adverse inference need only show that its opponent "knew of (a) the claim (that is, the litigation or the potential for litigation), and (b) the document's potential relevance to that claim." If that showing is made, then "a trier of fact may (but need not) infer from a party's obliteration of a document relevant to a litigated issue that the contents of the document were unfavorable to that party."

b.   Degree of Prejudice

Prejudice or harm from spoliation occurs when the requesting party is unable to obtain production of relevant information that would have helped its case because the information was destroyed in violation of a legal duty to preserve. However, it is not easy to demonstrate the relevance of information that no longer exists. In *Residential Funding*, discussed earlier, the court held that when the loss of

evidence is caused by reckless or intentional conduct, that conduct alone is sufficient to establish a
presumption of relevance. However, if the loss of
evidence is caused by negligence, or even gross
negligence, then the proponent of an adverse inference charge has the burden of proving that the
missing evidence would have been relevant. *See
Zubulake v. UBS Warburg LLC ("Zubulake IV"),*
220 F.R.D. 212 (S.D.N.Y. 2003) (denying plaintiff's
request for an adverse inference because plaintiff
had only shown that the loss of evidence resulted
from defendant's negligence or gross negligence
and was unable to show the relevance of the lost
information). As a result, circumstantial evidence is
often necessary to establish the relevance of the altered or destroyed evidence, and the resulting prejudice caused by its loss.

i. Prejudice as a Necessary Element of Spoliation

In *Greyhound Lines, Inc. v. Wade,* 485 F.3d 1032
(8th Cir. 2007), a bus company sued the driver of a
delivery truck alleging that the truck rear-ended
the bus. Defendant appealed the judgment, asserting that the trial court erred in refusing to sanction
plaintiff for the loss of some data stored in an
electronic control module ("ECM") that would have
helped establish that when the bus was struck it
was traveling below the posted speed limit. The
trial court found that defendant had suffered no
prejudice because the ECM data that had been

preserved identified the specific mechanical defect that slowed the bus, and several bus passengers testified as to how the bus was driven before the collision. The court concluded—and the appeals court affirmed—that "[t]here must be a finding of prejudice to the opposing party before imposing a sanction for destruction of evidence."

ii. Circumstantial Evidence of Prejudice

Courts have recognized the inherent problem in requiring a party to show prejudice from spoliation when the necessary evidence is, by definition, missing. To require too specific a showing would reward the spoliator. Thus, courts have often lowered the bar, for example, by holding that the complete destruction of the evidence justifies a finding of prejudice.

In some situations, it may be possible to demonstrate the prejudicial effect of spoliation using information that was preserved and produced, and that shows the likely relevance and impact of the destroyed information. For instance, in the *Zubulake* case, plaintiff eventually was able to establish the relevance of the missing e-mails because she had made and kept printouts of approximately 450 e-mails related directly to the issues in the case which established that the missing e-mails would have been relevant.

In other cases, it may be possible to extract the lost information from other sources, albeit at great expense and with the aid of computer forensics; for example, where a witness deleted e-mails from a laptop, they may be recoverable by forensic examination of the computer's hard drive. Courts may appoint an independent expert to ensure that all steps are being taken to recover missing information. For example, in *Keir v. UnumProvident Corp.*, 2003 WL 21997747 (S.D.N.Y. Aug. 22, 2003), where defendant failed to comply with a preservation order and overwrote certain backup tapes subject to the order, the court recognized that "[h]ow much has been lost, and the extent of prejudice to the plaintiffs from the loss cannot be determined at this time" and appointed an independent expert to determine whether appropriate efforts were underway to retrieve the e-mail lost from the destroyed backup tapes.

iii.   Standard of Proof Needed to Establish Prejudice

In *Micron Technology, Inc. v. Rambus, Inc.*, 255 F.R.D. 135 (D. Del. 2009), a patent enforceability action, the court noted that the burden of proof necessary to establish spoliation was not settled in the Third Circuit. The court noted that the standard is understandably flexible, requiring only "a reasonable possibility, based on concrete evidence" that the spoliated evidence would have been relevant and material. Nonetheless, the court noted that "clear and convincing" evidence is needed to justify a dispositive sanction. The court then proposed balancing the standard of proof to establish *intent* with the standard of proof to establish *prejudice*. "[O]nce intent and prejudice have been established, the court must determine whether their total weight satisfies the clear and convincing standard of proof. In this regard, the showing of intent (i.e., bad faith) can be proportionally less when balanced against high prejudice. In contrast, the showing of intent must be proportionally greater when balanced against low prejudice." The court found that defendant had destroyed evidence in bad faith, that plaintiff had demonstrated the requisite "reasonable possibility, based on concrete evidence" to establish prejudice, and that defendant's litigation conduct was "obstructive at best, misleading at worst." As a sanction, the court held that defendant's patents were unenforceable against plaintiff.

iv. Presumption of Prejudice Based on Intentional Misconduct

In many situations, however, it is not possible either to determine the likely contents of the destroyed information or extract it from another source through no fault of the requesting party. Accordingly, as noted earlier, courts will presume prejudice where the culpability of the spoliator is egregious—namely reckless or intentional. In such cases, courts will look to remedial sanctions to put the requesting party in the position it would have been in had the spoliation not occurred. The degree of prejudice or harm will always impact the nature and severity of sanctions. Where the prejudice is very great, the assessment of the spoliator's culpability becomes less important. It is fair to say that the appropriate sanction turns on the facts of each case, both with respect to culpability and prejudice.

2.   Rule 37(e)

When first proposed, Rule 37(e) was regarded as a "safe harbor" from discovery sanctions that might arise from the routine deletion of information from computer systems. But it is not obvious that Rule 37(e) affords certain protection against sanctions. Indeed, it has been rarely relied on (either pro or con) and its sparse language raises serious questions about its reach and scope. It is useful to carefully review its 36 words:

- **'Absent exceptional circumstances** ...' Although not explicit, there is general acceptance that "exceptional circumstances" refers to exceptionally prejudicial loss of evidence.

- **'... a court may not impose sanctions under these rules** ...' A judge always has inherent authority or contempt powers.

- **'... on a party** ...' This phrase explicitly excludes the non-party served with a subpoena *duces tecum* for ESI under Rule 45.

- **'... for failing to provide electronically stored information lost as a result of the routine, good-faith operation** ...' The party seeking to avoid sanctions under this Rule

must provide evidence that the actions it took
were routine and in good faith.

- '. . . **of an electronic information system.**'
  This element focuses the inquiry on the system,
  and raises the question of whether human intervention or other external forces resulted in
  the loss of ESI.

a. "Good Faith"

Good faith is difficult to establish, but "bad
faith" is easier to demonstrate. *In re Krause*, 367
B.R. 740 (D. Kan. 2007), provides an example of a
decision finding that a party destroyed ESI in bad
faith. Krause was an adversary proceeding brought
by the Government and joined by the trustee in a
bankruptcy matter, to recover assets from Krause.
Both the trustee and the Government sought sanctions against Krause for violation of a preliminary
injunction and discovery orders. The court found
that Krause had used wiping software on his computer, after the duty to preserve had attached.
Later, after Krause's computers had crashed while
the adversary proceeding was pending and document requests had been served, Krause resumed
using the wiping software in the restoration process. These findings led the court to the "inescap-
able conclusion" that Krause "willfully and intentionally destroyed" ESI.

The court also rejected Krause's attempt to seek
protection from Rule 37(e):

The undisputed evidence established that Krause's hard drives were far from being at full capacity thus making it improbable that electronic information was being overwritten or deleted by routine operation of his computers. Just as a litigant may have an obligation to suspend certain features of a "routine operation," the Court concludes that a litigant has an obligation to suspend features of a computer's operation that are not routine if those features will result in destroying evidence. Here, that obligation required Krause to disable the running of the wiping feature of GhostSurf as soon as the preservation duty attached. And it certainly obligated Krause to refrain from reinstalling GhostSurf when his computers crashed and he restored them.

Evidence adduced from salvaged ESI demonstrated to the *Krause* court that the destroyed ESI would have been relevant and that the Government and the trustee had been significantly prejudiced. The court entered a partial default judgment against Krause.

b. "Routine Operation"

In *Doe v. Norwalk Community College*, 248 F.R.D. 372 (D. Conn. 2007), plaintiff in a discrimination action obtained an order allowing her expert to inspect some of the College's computers. The expert concluded that several of the hard drives had been "wiped" and were "totally devoid of data."

Additionally, the expert found that four electronic mailboxes had inconsistencies "that indicate that data has been altered, destroyed or filtered." Although the state college was subject to the state's document retention policy, the College's IT technician testified that he did not consider that it applied to "normal computer usage" or e-mail messages. The court held that the College could not take advantage of Rule 37(e)'s safe harbor against sanctions for the loss of discoverable ESI for two reasons. *First*, "in order to take advantage of the good faith exception, a party needs to act affirmatively to prevent the system from destroying or altering information, even if such destruction would occur in the regular course of business. Because the defendants failed to suspend [the system], the defendants cannot take advantage of Rule 37(e)'s good faith exception." *Second*, the court found that "the Rule only applies to information lost due to the 'routine operation of an electronic information system'. . . . This Rule therefore appears to require a routine system in order to take advantage of the good faith exception, and the court cannot find that the defendants had such a system in place."

A different result was reached in *Escobar v. City of Houston*, 2007 WL 2900581 (S.D. Tex. Sept. 29, 2007). In that case, plaintiffs alleged that the City had failed to preserve electronic communications by the Houston Police Department in the twenty-four hours after the shooting death of a minor. Plaintiffs alleged that they had provided notice to the City of their wrongful death claim within sixty days after the shooting and that the electronic communications were likely to discuss events that occurred after the minor had been shot. Police department policy was to keep transmissions for ninety days. Plaintiffs argued that the destruction of these communications violated the City's preservation obligation and sought an adverse inference instruction.

The City argued that plaintiffs' notice of claim did not specifically request all electronic communications, that it was unaware that plaintiffs sought the electronic communications, and that it preserved all evidence it *believed* to be relevant. The court noted that "[I]n the Fifth Circuit, a severe sanction for spoliation, including an adverse inference instruction, requires a showing of bad faith." The court found that absent proof of relevance or bad faith the routine and automatic destruction of the police department's electronic communications was not sanctionable. The court further found that the electronic communications were destroyed in the routine operation of defendant's computer system, and sanctions were therefore precluded under Rule 37(e).

c. Other Decisions Citing Rule 37(e)

Although Rule 37(e) does not explicitly address the duty to preserve, two courts have cited it as instructive in that regard. In *State of Texas v. City of Frisco*, 2008 WL 828055 (E.D. Tex. Mar. 27, 2008), plaintiff sought a declaratory judgment that it need not preserve ESI based on a letter request it received from the City. Plaintiff sought relief under the Declaratory Judgment Act. In dismissing the complaint, the court held that the letter from the City, which requested the general preservation of ESI pertaining to a toll road project and referred only to potential litigation, was insufficient to "rise to the level of controversy sufficient to confer jurisdiction." The court did note, however, citing to Rule 37, that while the Rules do not specifically address pre-suit litigation hold requests, they contemplate that the parties will act in good faith in the preservation and production of documents, and encourage the parties "to handle the preservation of documents in response to their respective litigation holds in such good faith." *State of Texas* suggests that Rule 37(e) might indicate the extent of a pre-litigation duty to preserve and might impose a pre-litigation good faith standard, providing some additional guidance to consideration of the common law duty to preserve.

A Sixth Circuit decision, *John B. v. Goetz*, 531 F.3d 448 (6th Cir. 2008), recognized Rule 37(e)'s relationship to the well-established principle that "a party to civil litigation has a duty to preserve relevant information, including ESI, when that party 'has notice that the evidence is relevant to litigation or . . . should have known that the evidence may be relevant to future litigation.'" When this duty to preserve the relevant data is breached, "a . . . court may exercise its authority to impose appropriate discovery sanctions." The court noted that sanctions should only be considered when there is a clear duty to preserve ESI, a culpable failure to preserve and produce relevant ESI, and a reasonable probability of material prejudice to the adverse party.

In *John B.*, the Sixth Circuit granted in part the mandamus petition of defendants, officials of the State of Tennessee responsible for the operation of that state's managed health care system. The district court had required the forensic imaging and production of hard drives and other devices of a number of state personnel despite confidentiality and privacy concerns. The Court of Appeals held that these concerns (confidentiality and privacy), together with federal and comity concerns, warranted mandamus relief from the district court's order. As with *State of Texas*, the reference to Rule 37(e) in *John B.* is fleeting. The Rule is cited solely in reference to the duty to preserve relevant information and a court's authority to impose appropriate sanctions.

3. Appropriate Sanctions

Just as culpable conduct and prejudice are defined along a sliding scale, so is the range of sanctions that a court can impose. Those sanctions include: fines, cost-shifting, burden shifting, preclusion of evidence, adverse inferences, and default judgments. Most courts are careful to impose the least severe sanctions commensurate with the wrongdoing.

For example, in *Metropolitan Opera Association, Inc. v. Local 100, Hotel Employees and Restaurant Employees International Union*, 212 F.R.D. 178 (S.D.N.Y. 2003), the judge considered the range of possible sanctions under a particularly egregious set of circumstances. After reviewing the discovery failures and abuses in great detail, the court entered a default judgment "in order to (1) remedy the effect of the discovery abuses, *viz.*, prejudicing [plaintiff]'s ability to plan and prepare its case, (2) punish the parties responsible, and (3) deter similar conduct by others." In rejecting any lesser sanction the court noted that "because of the egregiousness of the conduct at issue and because it continued in the face of repeated, documented examples of non-compliance and repeated inquiries by [plaintiff's] counsel and the Court, a lesser sanction would not be adequate to penalize the [defendant] and its counsel here or to deter others from similar misconduct in the future."

a.   Default Judgment or Dismissal

A district court may order a default judgment or a dismissal, either pursuant to Rule 37(b)(2), which authorizes a court to assess a sanction for violation of a discovery order, or pursuant to the court's inherent power to protect its integrity and prevent abuses of the judicial process. When evaluating the propriety of dismissal or default as a discovery sanction, a court should consider: (1) the degree of actual prejudice to the other party; (2) the amount of interference with the judicial process; (3) the culpability of the litigant; (4) whether the court warned the party in advance that default or dismissal of the action would be a likely sanction for noncompliance; and (5) the efficacy of lesser sanctions.

b. Adverse Inference Jury Instruction

When a party fails to produce relevant evidence within its control, that failure may permit a court to instruct the jury that it may infer that the missing evidence is unfavorable to the party. An adverse inference can be drawn only if the party had control of the evidence that was lost.

When a party has destroyed relevant evidence, an inference that the evidence would have been unfavorable to the party arises. A party seeking such a "spoliation" adverse inference must adduce sufficient evidence from which a reasonable juror could infer the unfavorable nature of the destroyed evidence. As noted earlier, relevance will be presumed if the loss of evidence is due to reckless or intentional misconduct. Otherwise, the proponent of the adverse inference instruction bears the burden of proving that the lost evidence would have been relevant.

It is also interesting to note that unlike all other sanctions that a court can impose, the court does not have the last word with respect to the impact of the sanction. *See Nucor Corp. v. Bell*, 251 F.R.D. 191, 203 (D.S.C. 2008) (noting that even after the court has decided that the spoliating party's conduct warrants an adverse inference instruction, the jury must still decide whether to draw the adverse inference against that party). The jury is required to make the following findings before drawing the inference that the lost evidence would have been unfavorable to the party that caused the loss: (1) the party caused the loss; (2) the evidence was within that party's control; and (3) the lost evidence would have been material in deciding the dispute. Even then, the jury is *permitted*, but not *required*, to infer that the evidence would have been unfavorable to the party that caused its loss. *See Zubulake v. UBS Warburg LLC ("Zubulake V")*, 229 F.R.D. 422 (S.D.N.Y. 2004) ("If you find that: (1) [defendant] could have produce this evidence; (2) the evidence was within its control; and (3) the evidence would have been material in deciding facts in dispute in this case, you are *permitted, but not required,* to infer that the evidence would have been unfavorable to [defendant].").

c. Monetary Sanctions

Sanctions against a spoliator may include reimbursement of attorneys fees, monetary penalties against the party or attorney, and recovery of discovery costs. For example, in *Doctor John's, Inc. v. City of Sioux City, Iowa*, 486 F. Supp. 2d 953 (N.D. Iowa 2007), plaintiff sued the City over an ordinance restricting adult entertainment establishments. While the suit was settled, the court retained jurisdiction "over the question of whether or not sanctions should be imposed upon the City for destruction, during the pendency of litigation, of relevant records, which consisted of recordings of closed sessions of the City Council concerning the ordinances challenged in this case." The court found that the City had engaged in sanctionable misconduct and imposed a monetary sanction of $50,000.

While reimbursement of attorneys' fees and monetary penalties may constitute a sanction,[2] shifting of discovery costs might be considered more of a case management consideration under Rule 26(c)(1)(B) and Rule 26(c)(2). These rules provide that a court may "specify the terms" for discovery or disclosure and may "on just terms" order that "a party or person provide or permit discovery."

d.   Who Is Subject to Sanctions?

Although Rule 37 speaks of sanctioning "a party," courts generally do not sanction a party where the fault lies with inattentive, inept, or incompetent counsel. Because sanctions are based on personal responsibility, where counsel alone is responsible, counsel alone should be sanctioned. However, circumstances may demand that both party and counsel be held responsible.

In *In re September 11th Liability Insurance Coverage Cases*, 243 F.R.D. 114 (S.D.N.Y. 2007), the

2. *See, e.g.*, Fed. R. Civ. P. 26(g)(3).

court sanctioned an insurer for the untimely production of relevant documents, including a printed copy of a policy as it existed on the day of the occurrence, an attached endorsement affecting the additional insured status of the litigants, and other requested materials. The court found the insurer had deleted an electronic copy of the policy as it appeared in its computer records. The court also found that the insurer's attorneys allowed a printed copy of the policy to languish in their files. The court imposed sanctions in the amount of $500,000 against the insurer and its attorneys jointly and severally, payable to the opposing party to defray the costs it had incurred in wasted discovery proceedings.

Where it is apparent that both the party and its counsel engaged in discovery misconduct, or the party and its counsel blame each other, the court is put in a difficult situation. *Qualcomm, Inc. v. Broadcom Corp.*, 2008 WL 66932 (S.D. Cal. Jan. 7, 2008), provides an example of this dilemma. In the final hours of this patent infringement trial involving digital video compression technology, cross-examination of a witness for plaintiff revealed that twenty-one highly relevant e-mails had not been produced during discovery. At the conclusion of the trial, the jury returned a verdict for defendant, and counsel for defendant filed a motion for sanctions. In post-verdict discovery, Qualcomm produced more than 46,000 documents which had been requested but not previously produced, in addition to the twenty-one revealed at trial. The court found that there is clear and convincing evidence that [plaintiff] intentionally engaged in conduct designed to prevent [defendant] from learning [of certain evidence]. To this end, [plaintiff] withheld tens of thousands of emails ... and then utilized [defendant's] lack of access to the suppressed evidence to repeatedly and falsely aver that there was "no evidence" [of its culpable conduct]. [Plaintiff]'s misconduct in hiding the emails and electronic documents prevented [defendant] from correcting the false statements and countering the misleading arguments.

However, the court referred to the Magistrate Judge the question of what role in the discovery misconduct, if any, was played by Qualcomm's outside counsel. The court found

one or more of the retained lawyers chose not to look in the correct locations for the correct documents, to accept the unsubstantiated assurances of an important client that its search was sufficient, to ignore the warning signs that the document search and production were inadequate, not to press [plaintiff's] employees for the truth, and/or to encourage employees to provide the information (or lack of information).... These choices enabled [plaintiff] to withhold hundreds of thousands of pages of relevant discovery and to assert numerous false and misleading arguments to the court and jury. This conduct warrants the imposition of sanctions.

The court ordered Qualcomm to pay more than $8.5 million in attorneys' fees and costs, and ordered both Qualcomm and its outside attorneys to "participate in a ... process to identify the failures in the case management and discovery protocol utilized by Qualcomm and its in-house and retained attorneys in this case, to craft alternatives that will prevent such failures in the future, to evaluate and test the alternatives, and ultimately, to create a case management protocol which will serve as a model for the future." In addition, Qualcomm's outside attorneys were ordered to report themselves to the California State Bar.

Qualcomm's outside attorneys were hampered by the California Rules of Professional Conduct in shielding themselves against the imposition of sanctions because these Rules prevented the attorneys from disclosing client communications in their own defense. The sanctioned lawyers appealed. The district judge vacated the Magistrate Judge's order in part, holding that the attorney-client privilege should not have prevented the attorneys from using client communications to defend themselves and remanded the case as to the individual attorneys for another hearing. Importantly, the court did not question the appropriateness of sanctions against the lawyers if the facts were as the Magistrate Judge had found them to be, and the court affirmed the sanctions against Qualcomm.

CHAPTER VII

ETHICAL ISSUES IN E–DISCOVERY

This chapter discusses several ethical issues that commonly arise in electronic discovery. These issues are disclosure and use of metadata; duties of candor, competence and fairness; and supervision of the activities of clients, subordinate attorneys, and non-attorneys.

The American Bar Association's Model Rules of Professional Conduct ("ABA Model Rules") are generally the starting point of any discussion involving legal ethics and the standards of professional responsibility for lawyers. Almost all states use the ABA Model Rules as the basis for their state ethics rules; various courts rely on them in resolving cases of lawyer malpractice.[1] However, reliance on the ABA Model Rules has not resulted in uniformity of opinion on the ethical issues discussed in this chapter, and the reader is urged to consult the opinions

---

1. To date, only California and Maine do not have professional conduct rules that follow the format of the ABA Model Rules. Effective April 1, 2009, New York shifted to the Model Rules from the predecessor ABA Model Code of Professional Responsibility. Also note that because these are "model" rules, the rules in states which do follow the ABA may vary from the model rules. *See* http://www.abanet.org/cpr/mrpc/model_rules.html.

of ethics authorities in each jurisdiction for guidance on these issues.

A. METADATA

Chapter V discusses the issues associated with the discoverability of metadata. This chapter will address the ethical obligations imposed on lawyers when producing and reviewing metadata embedded within ESI. Divergent opinions have emerged regarding the following key issues:

1. Does a sending attorney have an affirmative duty to ensure that a client's confidential metadata are properly protected from inadvertent or inappropriate disclosure?

2. Does an attorney have an affirmative obligation to preserve and produce a client's relevant metadata in response to a discovery request?

3. Is it unethical for an attorney receiving ESI from opposing counsel to review or "mine" the ESI for metadata?

1. Ethical Concerns for the Producing Attorney
a. Attorney's Duty to Maintain Client Confidences

Attorneys routinely engage in transactional activities, such as negotiating contracts or drafting agreements, where communications containing metadata are exchanged with other parties and their counsel. Both the ABA and state bar association opinions agree that attorneys owe a duty to use reasonable care to guard against the disclosure of metadata containing confidential information and a duty to provide competent representation. Support is found in Rules 1.1 and 1.6(a) of the ABA Model Rules.

Rule 1.1: A lawyer shall provide competent representation to a client. Competent representation requires the legal knowledge, skill, thoroughness and preparation reasonably necessary for the representation.

Rule 1.6(a): A lawyer shall not reveal information relating to the representation of a client unless the client gives informed consent, the disclosure is impliedly authorized in order to carry out the representation or the disclosure is permitted by [the Rule].

Comment [17]: When transmitting a communication that includes information relating to the representation of a client, the lawyer must take reasonable precautions to prevent the information from coming into the hands of unintended recipients. This duty, however, does not require that the lawyer use special security measures if the method of communication affords a reasonable expectation of privacy. Special circumstances, however, may warrant special precautions. Factors to be considered in determining the reasonableness of the lawyer's expectation of confidentiality include the sensitivity of the information and the extent to which the privacy of the communication is protected by law or by a confidentiality agreement. . . .

District of Columbia Ethics Opinion 341 (2007), entitled "Review and Use of Metadata in Electronic Documents," states that "[l]awyers sending electronic documents outside of the context of responding to discovery or subpoenas have an obligation under Rule 1.6 to take reasonable steps to maintain the confidentiality of documents in their possession." Several other state ethics bodies have issued similar opinions, including Colorado, Maryland, Arizona, Alabama, and New York.

Opinion 06–442 from the ABA's Standing Committee on Ethics and Professional Responsibility discusses steps attorneys should take when sending information containing metadata.

ABA Formal Opinion 06–442: Review and Use of Metadata

The Committee observes that counsel sending or producing electronic documents may be able to limit the likelihood of transmitting metadata in electronic documents. Computer users can avoid creating some kinds of metadata in electronic documents in the first place. For example, they often can choose not to use the redlining function of a word processing program or not to embed comments in a document. Simply deleting comments might be effective to eliminate them. Computer users also can eliminate or "scrub" some kinds of embedded information in an electronic document before sending, producing, or providing it to others.* * *

A lawyer who is concerned about the possibility of sending, producing, or providing to opposing counsel a document that contains or might contain metadata also may be able to send a different version of the document without the embedded information. For example, she might send it in hard copy, create an image of the document and send only the image (this can be done by printing and scanning), or print it out and send it via facsimile.

b. Attorney's Duties With Respect to Discovery

Once a case enters the discovery phase, attorneys must balance the duty to maintain client confidences under the Model Rules with the requirements of the discovery rules. ABA Model Rule 3.4 provides that attorneys owe a duty of fairness to the opposing party and counsel.

Rule 3.4: A lawyer shall not: (a) unlawfully obstruct another party's access to evidence or unlawfully alter, destroy or conceal a document or other material having potential evidentiary value. A lawyer shall not counsel or assist another person to do any such act.

Common law obligates an attorney to preserve relevant evidence.

D.C. Bar Ethics Opinion 341: Because it is impermissible to alter electronic documents that constitute tangible evidence, the removal of metadata may, at least in some instances, be prohibited as well. In addition to issues regarding discovery sanctions, the alteration or destruction of evidence can, under some circumstances, also constitute a crime.

Therefore, while an attorney's duty to maintain client confidence may have required her to "scrub" metadata from documents generated in the transactional setting, the attorney's duty of fairness to the opposing party and counsel may require her to preserve metadata associated with client documents once litigation is reasonably anticipated. However, the duty to preserve and produce metadata are constrained by considerations of relevance and privilege.

Williams v. Sprint/United Management Co., 230 F.R.D. 640 (D. Kan. 2005), was one of the first cases to discuss the obligation to produce metadata in substantial detail. It did not discuss ethical issues directly, but shed considerable light on the contours of the obligation to preserve and produce metadata. *Williams* held that "when a party is ordered to produce electronic documents as they are maintained in the ordinary course of business, the producing party should produce the electronic documents with their metadata intact, unless that party timely objects to production of metadata." *Wyeth v. Impax Laboratories, Inc.*, 248 F.R.D. 169 (D. Del. 2006), decided a year after *Williams*, announced a different standard. The *Wyeth* court supported a presumption against the production of metadata,

which can be overcome only if the metadata are
deemed to be relevant, non-privileged, and reasonably accessible. These two decisions, and the many
others regarding the production of metadata, demonstrate that metadata cannot be treated categori-
cally. A more detailed discussion regarding the need
to produce metadata is found in Chapter V.D, *supra*.

"Sending" attorneys must exercise caution in
producing ESI containing metadata during discovery. Inadvertent disclosure of privileged information—which can be found in metadata—may be
detrimental to a case. Although a producing party
may have a duty to produce metadata if relevant
and non-privileged, attorneys still have an obligation to protect a client's confidential information.
Like all other forms of ESI, metadata must be
reviewed before a decision can be made as to
whether it must be preserved as potential evidence,
produced in discovery, withheld on the basis of
privilege, or disposed of in the ordinary course of
business.

2. Ethical Concerns for the Receiving At-
torney

The ethical dilemmas surrounding metadata are
not the exclusive province of the producing attorney. The attorney who receives ESI from opposing
counsel also faces ethical issues in regards to metadata.

"Mining metadata" refers to the practice of searching a document's underlying metadata for hidden or embedded information. There are conflicting answers to the question of whether metadata mining violates an attorney's ethical obligations. The views range from "mining is ethical" to "it is completely unethical." Generally, the debate surrounding the answer stems from differing interpretations of ABA Model Rule 4.4(b) and analogous state rules.

Rule 4.4(b): A lawyer who receives a document relating to the representation of the lawyer's client and knows or reasonably should know that the document was inadvertently sent shall promptly notify the sender.

Comment 2: Paragraph (b) recognizes that lawyers sometimes receive documents that were mistakenly sent or produced by opposing parties or their lawyers. If a lawyer knows or reasonably should know that such a document was sent inadvertently, then this Rule requires the lawyer to promptly notify the sender in order to permit that person to take protective measures. Whether the lawyer is required to take additional steps, such as returning the original document, is a matter of law beyond the scope of these Rules, as is the question of whether the privileged status of a document has been waived. . . .

a. Decisions Holding that Mining of Metadata Is Unethical

New York was among the first jurisdictions to address the ethical obligations of attorneys in relation to metadata. The New York State Bar Committee on Professional Ethics issued Opinion 749 in 2001 stating that it is unethical for attorneys to mine metadata, reasoning that the information found "may be protected by the attorney-client privilege, the work product doctrine or … may otherwise constitute a 'secret' of another lawyer's client [that] would violate the letter and spirit of these Disciplinary Rules." The bar associations of Florida, Alabama, and Arizona have taken a similar position on mining metadata.

b. Decisions Holding that Mining Metadata Is Ethical

In August 2006, the ABA's Standing Committee on Ethics and Professional Responsibility ("Standing Committee") issued Opinion 06–442. Unlike New York, the ABA found that the Model Rules did not contain any specific provisions that would forbid attorneys from reviewing and using metadata. It held that Rule 4.4(b) is silent as to whether a lawyer may ethically review or use such information. The Rule provides only that "a lawyer who receives a document relating to the representation of the lawyer's client and knows or reasonably should know that the document was inadvertently sent shall promptly notify the sender."

Jurisdictions that have not addressed the ethical implications of mining metadata generally use the ABA's advisory opinion as guidance in their disciplinary actions. Even though the ABA's formal opinions do not carry precedential weight, courts look to them for advice in interpreting the Model Rules that most attorneys are required to follow.

c. Hybrid Decisions

A number of states have chosen an in-between approach to the question of metadata mining. Instead of placing an absolute bar on this activity, these opinions carve out situations where lawyers can ethically look at metadata. D.C. Legal Ethics Opinion 341 (2007) states that a "receiving lawyer is prohibited from reviewing metadata sent by an adversary only where he has *actual knowledge* that the metadata was inadvertently sent." In 2008, the Colorado Bar Association Ethics Committee held that a receiving lawyer generally may review metadata unless he knows or reasonably should know that the metadata contain confidential information, in which case he should assume that it was transmitted inadvertently. In that instance, he must then notify the sending attorney of the inadvertent production.

B. DUTIES OF CANDOR, COMPETENCE AND FAIRNESS

1. Introduction

Electronic discovery has significantly changed the way counsel (in-house and outside) interact with their clients when litigation is pending or threatened. Lawyers are now required to take affirmative roles in advising their clients regarding the identification, preservation, collection and production of ESI. These lawyers also may have to confront two potentially countervailing interests—their obligations to their clients and their ethical duties as officers of the court. While this dilemma is certainly not new to attorneys, the age of electronic discovery has added a new twist to the tension between these two obligations. This section identifies ethical concerns that lawyers face regarding their duties of candor, competence, and fairness to the court and opposing counsel when confronting electronic discovery, and concludes with a discussion of the ethics of cooperative, non-adversarial discovery.

2. Duty of Candor

ABA Model Rule: 3.3 Candor Toward the Tribunal

(a) A lawyer shall not knowingly:

(1) make a false statement of fact or law to a tribunal or fail to correct a false statement of

material fact or law previously made to the tribunal by the lawyer;

* * *

(3) offer evidence that the lawyer knows to be false. If a lawyer, the lawyer's client, or a witness called by the lawyer, has offered material evidence and the lawyer comes to know of its falsity, the lawyer shall take reasonable remedial measures, including, if necessary, disclosure to the tribunal. A lawyer may refuse to offer evidence, other than the testimony of a defendant in a criminal matter, that the lawyer reasonably believes is false.

(b) A lawyer who represents a client in an adjudicative proceeding and who knows that a person intends to engage, is engaging or has engaged in criminal or fraudulent conduct related to the proceeding shall take reasonable remedial measures, including, if necessary, disclosure to the tribunal.

(c) The duties stated in paragraphs (a) and (b) continue to the conclusion of the proceeding, and apply even if compliance requires disclosure of information otherwise protected by Rule 1.6.

The lawyer's duty of candor plays an extremely important role in litigation. The legal system mandates that lawyers, as officers of the court, present information in a truthful manner because judges, juries, and opposing counsel rely on this information to make factual and legal decisions. Without the duty of candor, the integrity of the adjudicative process would be severely undermined.

With the explosion of the use of ESI in business and in litigation, new and experienced attorneys must familiarize themselves not only with the changes to federal and state rules regarding e-discovery but must also immerse themselves in the technology in order to satisfy the required level of knowledge necessary to uphold their duty of candor. Recently, courts have levied significant sanctions against counsel for violating the duty of candor in cases involving discovery of ESI.

Violating this obligation can also pose serious danger to the client. Courts have issued adverse inference instructions to juries for violations by counsel of the duty of candor, in one case resulting in an award of over $1.5 billion (later overturned on appeal on unrelated grounds).[2]

When litigation is pending or threatened, lawyers must be very careful in performing due diligence in the identification, preservation, review and production of ESI to ensure that they are presenting truthful and accurate information to the court and the opposing parties. Attorneys who intentionally or unintentionally mislead a trier of fact or falsely certify compliance with a discovery order run the risk of compromising not only their clients' cases but in extreme cases, their professional careers.

2. *See Coleman (Parent) Holdings, Inc. v. Morgan Stanley & Co., Inc.*, 2005 WL 679071 (Fla. Cir. Ct. Mar. 1, 2005); *Coleman (Parent) Holdings, Inc. v. Morgan Stanley & Co., Inc.*, 2005 WL 674885 (Fla. Cir. Ct. Mar. 23, 2005).

3. Duty of Competence

ABA Model Rule: 1.1: A lawyer shall provide competent representation to a client. Competent representation requires the legal knowledge, skill, thoroughness and preparation reasonably necessary for the representation.

Comment [5]: Major litigation and complex transactions ordinarily require more extensive treatment than matters of lesser complexity and consequence. See Rule 1.2(c).

Lawyers have a responsibility to educate themselves and their clients about the new and pertinent legal and technical issues regarding electronic discovery. This is especially true with respect to an attorney's duty to assist the client in the process of identifying, preserving, reviewing, and producing ESI. This includes an obligation to seek, as part of the lawyer's due diligence, all relevant information, positive or otherwise, which may relate to the claims at issue. To do otherwise is an ethical violation.

ABA Model Rule 8.4 notes that it is professional misconduct for a lawyer to, among other things: "(c) engage in conduct involving dishonesty, fraud, deceit or misrepresentation; or (d) engage in conduct that is prejudicial to the administration of justice." And these obligations apply to all attorneys—litigation and corporate counsel, in-house and outside counsel—alike. In the new age of electronic information and discovery, lawyers must be prepared to act with "diligence and competence" and with a sense of urgency to meet the obligations created by the electronic discovery amendments to the Federal Rules.

Moreover, lawyers cannot relieve themselves of their ethical obligations by outsourcing the work associated with electronic discovery to a more technologically-savvy organization such as a vendor, without direct supervision. Attorneys have an obligation to monitor the discovery process and ensure that relevant non-privileged information is identified, preserved, reviewed and produced. For instance, Rule 26(f) mandates that a lawyer must understand and competently investigate the electronic storage systems used by her client so that the lawyer can properly participate in the Rule 26 conference.

Ensuring that discovery procedures are properly followed involves offering adequate advice and instructions to clients regarding their obligations in discovery. Courts have not shied away from penalizing parties and their lawyers who fail to competently handle their duties of electronic discovery. In its opinion in *Metropolitan Opera Association, Inc. v. Local 100, Hotel Employees and Restaurant Employees International Union*, 2004 WL 1943099 (S.D.N.Y. Aug. 27, 2004), the court warned that the "defendants and their counsel may not engage in parallel know-nothing, do-nothing, head-in-the sand behavior in an effort consciously to avoid knowledge of or responsibility for their discovery obligations and to obstruct plaintiff's wholly appropriate efforts to prepare its case." In another case, the court awarded defendant costs and attorneys' fees because "a reasonable inquiry by the plaintiff's counsel . . . would have alerted counsel that the plaintiff possessed electronic mail that fell within the scope of [defendant]'s document request."[3]

4. Duty of Fairness

ABA Model Rule: 3.4: A lawyer shall not: (a) unlawfully obstruct another party's access to evidence . . .

Comment [1]: The procedure of the adversary system contemplates that the evidence in a case is to be marshaled competitively by the contending parties. Fair competition in the adversary system is secured by prohibitions against destruction or concealment of evidence, improperly influencing witnesses, obstructive tactics in discovery procedure, and the like.

Comment [2]: Documents and other items of evidence are often essential to establish a claim or defense. Subject to evidentiary privileges, the right of an opposing party, including the government, to obtain evidence through discovery or subpoena is an important procedural right. The exercise of that right can be frustrated if relevant material is altered, concealed or destroyed.

3. *Invasion Media Commc'ns, Inc. v. Federal Ins. Co.*, 2004 WL 396037, at *8 (S.D.N.Y. Mar. 2, 2004).

In addition to upholding the duties of candor and competence, a lawyer must ensure that he fulfills his duty of fairness to the opposing party and counsel. As explained above, a lawyer cannot destroy or conceal evidence. This means that lawyers also have an ethical duty to produce all relevant non-privileged ESI to opposing counsel. The duty of fairness prohibits attorneys from withholding a "smoking gun" document simply because the information is harmful to his client's position.

5. The Sedona Conference® Cooperation Proclamation

The mandatory initial disclosure requirement of Rule 26(a) and the "meet and confer" requirement of Rule 26(f) are useful mechanisms for expediting discovery, reducing costs, and avoiding conflict, when carried out in the spirit of candor, competence, and fairness found in the rules of professional responsibility. Many thoughtful lawyers—and many clients—would like to go further. Looking at the examples of arbitration and mediation, they question why discovery must be an adversarial process. If the goal of discovery is to uncover facts to be used in settlement talks or at trial, it would seem wise to cooperate in the discovery process, and utilize advocacy and persuasion skills to argue the interpretation of the facts and the application of the facts to the law. Should an attorney's duty of zealous advocacy and loyalty to the client include getting the best result at a reasonable cost and within a reasonable time frame? In the summer of 2008, these questions led members of The Sedona Conference, many of whom are highly experienced lawyers and judges in the electronic discovery arena, to issue a "Cooperation Proclamation."

Faced with the question of whether the strategy of "cooperation" conflicts with an attorney's duty of "zealous advocacy," the Proclamation declared:

> Lawyers have twin duties of loyalty: While they are retained to be zealous advocates for their clients, they bear a professional obligation to conduct discovery in a diligent and candid manner. Their combined duty is to strive in the best interests of their clients to achieve the best results at a reasonable cost, with integrity and candor as officers of the court. Cooperation does not conflict with the advancement of their clients' interests—it enhances it. Only when lawyers confuse advocacy with adversarial conduct are these twin duties in conflict.

The concept of "zealous advocacy" has undergone significant modification since 1969, when the ABA promulgated the Model Code of Professional Responsibility, which provided in Canon 7 that an attorney owes a duty "to represent his client zealously within the bounds of the law." In 1983, the ABA revised the model ethical rules governing attorneys with the publication of the Model Rules of Professional Conduct. Unlike the 1969 Model Code, the 1983 Model Rules do not contain a provision expressly imposing on attorneys a duty of zealous advocacy, but instead calls for "diligent representation."

The Cooperation Proclamation acknowledges that the prevailing legal culture continues to view "zealous advocacy" as an ethical duty and that the call to cooperate in discovery is not likely to be accepted immediately by all attorneys.

The effort to change the culture of discovery from adversarial conduct to cooperation is not utopian. It is, instead, an exercise in economy and logic. Establishing a culture of cooperation will channel valuable advocacy skills toward interpreting the facts and arguing the appropriate application of law.

* * *

It is unrealistic to expect a *sua sponte* outbreak of pre-trial discovery cooperation. Lawyers frequently treat discovery conferences as perfunctory obligations. They may fail to recognize or act on opportunities to make discovery easier, less costly, and more productive. New lawyers may not yet have developed cooperative advocacy skills, and senior lawyers may cling to a long-held "hide the ball" mentality. Lawyers who recognize the value of resources such as ADR and special masters may nevertheless overlook their application to discovery. And, there remain obstreperous counsel with no interest in cooperation, leaving even the best-intentioned to wonder if "playing fair" is worth it.

To overcome the resistance to cooperation as a concept, and to provide concrete examples of ways opposing counsel can engage in cooperative discovery activities that result in lower costs and reduced burdens, The Sedona Conference intends to develop and publish cooperation principles and guidelines. Meanwhile, case law provides many illustrations of situations in which the parties could have saved time and money by cooperating.

In *Williams v. Taser International, Inc.*, 2007 WL 1630875 (N.D. Ga. June 4, 2007), the court "strongly encouraged the parties to collaborate on the development of search terms and a protocol for conducting . . . searches to winnow the universe of potentially responsive [electronic information]." The parties were unable to reach agreement and instead, each submitted a list of search terms for the court's consideration. Frustrated by the parties' inability to cooperate, the court issued an order imposing on the parties its own list of broad search terms. In so ordering, the court noted:

> The Court recognizes that the production ordered above will likely impose burdens on both parties. [Defendant] will likely be required to significantly increase its privilege review capabilities; Plaintiffs will likely be required to wade through a significant number of documents. Nevertheless, this case has been ongoing for more than 18 months, and yet discovery has progressed little and we remain far from its resolution. Because that is the case, and because the parties have been unable to cooperate

in the discovery process, the Court is compelled to Order the discovery procedures set forth above.

The parties' refusal to cooperate resulted in an aggravated judge and an order containing broad mandatory search terms likely to retrieve large volumes of information, which must then be reviewed thereby increasing the costs of litigation for both the defendant and the plaintiffs. But the court's order did not preclude future collaboration: "The parties may, by mutual agreement, develop and employ search protocols which vary from those set forth above. In the absence of such agreement, however, the production shall proceed in the manner described above."

A more positive example of judicial endorsement of the cooperation concept is provided by *Mancia v. Mayflower Textile Services Co.*, 253 F.R.D. 354 (D. Md. 2008), a wage-and-hour action brought by six hospital laundry workers against their employer that bogged down in a series of discovery disputes. In a lengthy and scholarly opinion, the judge cited the Cooperation Proclamation and other authorities for the proposition that cooperation with opposing counsel in discovery is a professional obligation, and that both sides must refrain from turning discovery into a tactical battleground. He ordered the parties to meet and confer to discuss the realistic damages alleged, estimate their attorney's fees in prosecuting and defending this action, and draft a discovery budget proportional to the issues in the case.

C. SUPERVISION, OUTSOURCING, LITIGATION SUPPORT, AND LAWYER ADJUNCTS

E-discovery requires a team effort. For example, litigants are well advised to create a "preservation triage team" of insiders who are familiar with the party's systems and operations and can act quickly to preserve appropriate materials. The preservation effort will often require the help of outside experts and litigation support personnel. Other professional teams may be necessary at later stages of discovery, particularly document review prior to production. But the team approach itself raises new issues. How should the e-discovery team be managed? Who is responsible for managing it? How should duties be allocated among the team members? Who has the final say between counsel and client? Who bears the ultimate responsibility for following court orders, complying with the Federal Rules of Civil Procedure, and upholding the Rules of Professional Conduct?

1. Obligations of Counsel

At the outset of litigation, to ensure that litigants comply with their preservation obligations, counsel should inform their clients: (1) of the existence of the duty to preserve information; (2) that the duty to preserve encompasses all "documents" potentially relevant to the dispute; and (3) that the definition of "document" encompasses hard copies and ESI, as well as drafts and non-identical copies.

Throughout the litigation, counsel may need to periodically remind their clients of the scope of the preservation requirement over the course of any litigation, or take other affirmative steps to monitor compliance.

Counsel's obligation continues through preservation and into the production phase. In *Board of Regents of University of Nebraska v. BASF Corp.*, 2007 WL 3342423 (D. Neb. Nov. 5, 2007), the court identified by name the attorney assigned to the task of managing discovery for the plaintiffs and described the lawyer's significant obligations:

> When faced with responding to a request for production of documents, counsel are required to direct the conduct of a thorough search for responsive documents. . . . Of course, when ordered by a court to produce documents, counsel are under an even higher obligation to affirmatively direct complete compliance with the order in . . . good faith. That standard was not met in this case. There is no evidence of any specific directives from counsel to the Board regarding what was required to ensure that all documents covered by the order were produced. . . . There is also no evidence of any assurances requested or given, sworn or otherwise, by University personnel to counsel to the effect that all covered documents had, in fact, been produced in accordance with the order. There is also no evidence of any directives given by counsel at any time for a "litigation

hold" to be placed on all relevant documents and electronically stored information. . . .

If counsel fail in this responsibility—willfully or not—[the] principles of an open discovery process are undermined, coextensively with inhibiting the courts' ability to objectively resolve their clients' disputes and the credibility of its resolution.

The failure of counsel to adequately oversee the preservation and discovery process may lead to the imposition of sanctions against the client. For example, in *Metropolitan Opera Association Inc. v. Local 100, Hotel Employees & Restaurant Employees International Union*, 212 F.R.D. 178 (S.D.N.Y. 2003), the court awarded sanctions against the defendant where its counsel:

(1) never gave adequate instructions to their clients about the clients' overall discovery obligations, [including a definition as to] what constitutes a "document" . . . ; (2) knew the [client] to have no document retention or filing systems and yet never implemented a systematic procedure for document production or for retention of documents, including electronic documents; (3) delegated document production to a layperson who . . . did not even understand himself (and was not instructed by counsel) that a document included a draft or other non-identical copy, a computer file and an e-mail; (4) never went back to the layperson designated to assure that he had "established[ed] a coherent

and effective system to faithfully and effectively respond to discovery requests," . . . and (5) in the face of the [plaintiff's] persistent questioning and showings that the production was faulty and incomplete, ridiculed the inquiries, failed to take any action to remedy the situation or supplement the demonstrably false responses, failed to ask important witnesses for documents until the night before their depositions and, instead, made repeated, baseless representations that all documents had been produced.

The court awarded a default judgment in favor of the plaintiff, reasoning that "it is impossible to know what the [plaintiff] would have found if the [defendant] and its counsel had complied with their discovery obligations from the commencement of the action."

2. Responsibility of Company Management

Responsibility for preservation and production of ESI also falls on the shoulders of a company's senior management. *In re Prudential Insurance Company of America Sales Practices Litigation*, 169 F.R.D. 598 (D.N.J. 1997), was a multidistrict litigation in which a communication breakdown between upper corporate management and the company's field offices resulted in the destruction of responsive documents at various locations. The court clearly blamed the company's leadership for the "haphazard and uncoordinated approach" to document preservation. The court stated:

[I]t became the obligation of senior management to initiate a comprehensive document preservation plan and to distribute it to all employees. Moreover, it was incumbent on senior management to advise its employees of the pending multi-district litigation ... to provide them with a copy of the Court's Order, and to acquaint its employees with the potential sanctions, both civil and criminal, that the Court could issue for noncompliance with this Court's Order.

When senior management fails to establish and distribute a comprehensive document retention policy, it cannot shield itself from responsibility because of field office actions. The obligation to preserve documents that are potentially discoverable materials is an affirmative one that rests squarely on the shoulders of senior corporate officers.

Similarly, in *Danis v. USN Communications, Inc.*, 2000 WL 1694325 (N.D. Ill. Oct. 20, 2000), the defendant's CEO delegated responsibility for document production to a new, in-house lawyer with no litigation experience. The Magistrate Judge recommended that the court fine the CEO $10,000 and issue a spoliation instruction.

3. Managing the Client-Lawyer Relationship

Counsel and client may not always agree on measures necessary to discharge the party's discovery obligations. Whose position should prevail? What can a lawyer do when faced with an obstinate client? In *Qualcomm Inc. v. Broadcom Corp.*, 2008 WL 66932 (S.D. Cal. Jan. 7, 2008), the Magistrate Judge took a tough stance:

> Leung's attorney represented during the OSC hearing that Leung [an attorney retained by Qualcomm] requested a more thorough document search but that Qualcomm refused to do so. If Leung was unable to get Qualcomm to conduct the type of search he deemed necessary to verify the adequacy of the document search and production, then he should have obtained the assistance of supervising or senior attorneys. If [the supervising attorneys] were unable to get Qualcomm to conduct a competent and thorough document search, they should have withdrawn from the case or taken other action to ensure production of the evidence.

The ABA Model Rules provide some guidelines for navigating the lawyer-client relationship. Rule 1.4 regarding Communications provides:

> (a) A lawyer shall:
>
> (1) promptly inform the client of any decision or circumstance with respect to which the client's informed consent ... is required by these Rules;
>
> (2) reasonably consult with the client about the means by which the client's objectives are to be accomplished; ...

(b) A lawyer shall explain a matter to the extent reasonably necessary to permit the client to make informed decisions regarding the representation.

Rule 1.2 regarding the Scope of Representation and Allocation of Authority Between Lawyer and Client provides:

(a) [A] lawyer shall abide by a client's decisions concerning the objectives of representation and ... shall consult with the client as to the means by which they are to be pursued.

4. Supervising Lawyers and Subordinates

In *Qualcomm*, the court found that each of several named attorneys "contributed to Qualcomm's monumental discovery violation and is personally responsible...." The sanctioned attorneys ranged from Qualcomm's lead attorney to a second-year associate who first discovered the responsive, unproduced e-mails. Regarding the responsibility of the junior associate, the court stated:

When [Associate] reviewed the August 6, 2002 email ... he knew or should have known that it contradicted Qualcomm's trial arguments and he had an obligation to verify that it had been produced in discovery or to immediately produce it. If [he], as a junior lawyer, lacked the experience to recognize the significance of the document, then a more senior or knowledgeable attorney should have assisted him. To the extent that [Partner] was supervising [Associate] in this endeavor, [Partner] certainly knew or should have recognized the importance of the document from his involvement in Qualcomm's motion practice and trial strategy sessions.

Similarly, when [Associate] found the 21 emails . . . that had not been produced in discovery, he took the appropriate action and informed his supervisors. . . .

The following ABA Model Rules address the relationship between supervising lawyers and subordinate lawyers.

Rule 5.1 Responsibilities of Partners, Managers, and Supervisory Lawyers

* * *

(b) A lawyer having direct supervisory authority over another lawyer shall make reasonable efforts to ensure that the other lawyer conforms to the Rules of Professional Conduct.

(c) A lawyer shall be responsible for another lawyer's violation of the Rules of Professional conduct if:

(1) the lawyer orders or, with knowledge of the specific conduct, ratifies the conduct involved; or

(2) the lawyer is a partner or has comparable managerial authority in the law firm in which the other lawyer practices, or has direct supervisory authority over the other lawyer, and

knows of the conduct at a time when its consequences can be avoided or mitigated but fails to take reasonable remedial action.

Rule 5.2 Responsibilities of a Subordinate Lawyer

(a) A lawyer is bound by the Rules of Professional Conduct notwithstanding that the lawyer acted at the direction of another person.

(b) A subordinate lawyer does not violate the Rules of Professional Conduct if that lawyer acts in accordance with a supervisory lawyer's reasonable resolution of an arguable question of professional duty.

Rule 5.2 Responsibilities of a Subordinate Lawyer—Comment [2]

When lawyers in a supervisor-subordinate relationship encounter a matter involving professional judgment as to ethical duty, the supervisor may assume responsibility for making the judgment. Otherwise a consistent course of action or position could not be taken. If the question can reasonably be answered only one way, the duty of both lawyers is clear and they are equally responsible for fulfilling it. However, if the question is reasonably arguable, someone has to decide upon the course of action. That authority ordinarily reposes in the supervisor, and a subordinate may be guided accordingly. . . .

a. Communication Is Critical

Qualcomm illustrates the critical importance of communication between counsel and client and among e-discovery and litigation team members. Knowledge may be imputed from client to counsel and from lawyer to associated lawyer whether or not it is actually communicated. A junior associate who is in charge of responding to discovery requests and preparing witnesses must communicate with the lead trial counsel who will be making arguments and representations in open court and at sidebar.

b. Lawyers and Consultants

Litigation support personnel, technology consultants and other outside experts play an important role on the e-discovery team. Such consultants are often non-lawyers. A supervising lawyer must ensure that all non-lawyers retained to assist with e-discovery conduct themselves in accordance with the Model Rules. Under some circumstances, the lawyer may even be held responsible for a non-lawyer's conduct. ABA Model Rule 5.3 provides:

With respect to a nonlawyer employed or retained by or associated with a lawyer:

(a) a partner, and a lawyer who individually or together with other lawyers possesses comparable managerial authority in a law firm shall make reasonable efforts to ensure that the firm has in effect measures giving reasonable assurance that the person's conduct is compatible with the professional obligations of the lawyer;

(b) a lawyer having direct supervisory authority over the nonlawyer shall make reasonable efforts to ensure that the person's conduct is compatible with the professional obligations of the lawyer; and

(c) a lawyer shall be responsible for conduct of such a person that would be a violation of the Rules of Professional Conduct if engaged in by a lawyer if:

(1) the lawyer orders or, with the knowledge of the specific conduct, ratifies the conduct involved; or

(2) the lawyer is a partner or has comparable managerial authority in the law firm in which the person is employed, or has direct supervisory authority over the person, and knows of the conduct at a time when its consequences can be avoided or mitigated but fails to take reasonable remedial action.

The comments to Rule 5.3 make clear that a lawyer must give consultants appropriate instruction and supervision concerning the ethical aspects of their employment and should keep in mind that non-lawyer consultants do not have legal training and are not subject to professional discipline. The Model Rule also imposes an obligation on law firms to design internal policies and procedures to ensure that non-lawyers also act in accordance with the Model Rules.

CHAPTER VIII

PRIVILEGE ISSUES ARISING DURING ELECTRONIC DISCOVERY

When lawyers produce information in response to a discovery demand, they must take care not to disclose their clients' privileged information. Such a disclosure could constitute a waiver of the privilege and, under some circumstances, might result in a finding of *subject matter waiver*—meaning that the client must make a further production of all privileged communications on the same subject matter as the previously disclosed documents. Therefore careful lawyers engage in pre-production review of documents to determine whether they are privileged.

While pre-production privilege review has always been necessary, the burdens of that review have skyrocketed in cases involving discovery of ESI—which is to say virtually all cases. The increasing volume of information and the various forms in which it is stored make privilege determinations more difficult. Similarly, privilege review is becoming more expensive and time-consuming, yet less likely to detect all privileged information. Typically, teams of lawyers (starting with contract lawyers

and subsequent reviews by junior and senior lawyers) read e-mails for hours on end, to determine
whether they contain privileged information. And of
course these e-mails all tend to look the same after
hours of review.

Fear of the consequences of mistaken disclosure
of privileged information—a phenomenon known as
inadvertent waiver—adds cost and delay to the discovery process for all parties. The risks inherent in
mistaken disclosures have been aggravated by some
decisions holding that a mistaken disclosure constitutes a subject matter waiver *regardless* of how
carefully the party tried to prevent the disclosure of
privileged information during discovery.

A. TEST FOR DETERMINING WAIVER BY MISTAKEN DISCLOSURE

Federal Rule of Evidence 502—enacted in September, 2008—provides some relief against waiver
by mistaken disclosure. Rule 502(b) provides that a
mistaken disclosure will not constitute a waiver if
the party took "reasonable steps" to prevent the
disclosure, and promptly rectified the error once it
discovered the mistake. This is essentially a negligence test. Rule 502(a) gives further protection by
providing that a mistaken disclosure in any federal
court proceeding or to any federal office or agency
can never justify a subject matter waiver—thus,
even if a party carelessly produces privileged information during discovery, the resulting waiver only
applies to the actual material disclosed. The party is

not required to make a further production of related privileged material.

What factors are relevant to whether a party took "reasonable steps" to avoid waiver by mistaken disclosure? Inherent in the word "reasonable" is a case-by case approach with no bright-line rules. Courts consider various relevant factors. One obvious consideration is the number of mistaken disclosures compared to the volume of information subject to review. If a party mistakenly disclosed only a small proportion of the documents reviewed, then the review process is more likely to be found reasonable than if the party disclosed a large number of privileged documents out of a relatively limited set of discoverable materials. Besides this proportional inquiry, other relevant factors include:

- The time constraints for production. If the party is subject to an accelerated deadline, privileged documents might slip past even a careful review.

- The use of analytical software and effective search terms. If the party reasonably uses search terms that are likely to find relevant data while screening out privileged documents, then employing that search terminology may show that the party took "reasonable steps" to prevent a mistaken disclosure.

- Implementation of an efficient system of records management before litigation arises. If the records system is well organized and data can be retrieved efficiently, the system itself is indicative of a reasonable effort to avoid a mistaken disclosure.

• Number of levels of review and personnel used to review the data. The greater the number of "eyes-on" review of the information before it is produced, the more likely that a court will find that the party took reasonable steps. And lawyers need to be involved in the review—leaving it to only IT people or paralegals is not reasonable.

In *Victor Stanley, Inc. v. Creative Pipe, Inc.*, 250 F.R.D. 251 (D. Md. 2008), a case that predated the adoption of Rule 502, the court held that the party that inadvertently produced privileged documents and then seeks their return has the burden of proving that its conduct in reviewing and producing documents was reasonable. The court in *Victor Stanley* found that defendants had failed to carry that burden. The court stated:

Defendants have failed to provide the court with information regarding: the keywords used; the rationale for their selection; the qualifications of M. Pappas and his attorneys to design an effective and reliable search and information retrieval method; whether the search was a simple keyword search, or a more sophisticated one, such as one employing Boolean proximity operators; or whether they analyzed the results of the search to assess its reliability, appropriateness for the task, and the quality of its implementation.

As a result, the court found that defendants' production of privileged documents resulted in a waiver.

B. AGREEMENTS BETWEEN PARTIES TO PROTECT AGAINST WAIVER BY DISCLOSURE IN DISCOVERY

While Rule 502(b) provides some basic protection against waiver by mistaken disclosure, the protection is indeterminate—there is no clear definition of the "reasonable steps" that must be taken to earn the protection, and each case must be decided on its circumstances. Parties understandably would like more predictability on whether a pre-production privilege review of ESI will sufficiently guard against waiver.

Consequently, parties often enter into agreements to control the risks of waiver when privileged ESI is disclosed during discovery. These agreements typically cover inadvertent disclosure, but can also cover intentional disclosures. Generally speaking there are two kinds of agreements: "quick peek" and "claw back." Under a "quick peek" agreement the producing party provides certain requested materials for initial examination, without waiving any privilege or protection. The requesting party then designates the documents it wishes to have produced. This designation is the Rule 34 request. The responding party then responds in the usual course, screening only those documents actually requested for formal production and asserting privilege claims as provided in Rule 26(b)(5)(A). Under a "claw back" agreement, a mistaken disclosure of privileged data is not deemed to be a waiver as long as the producing party identifies the documents mistakenly produced, and the documents must then be returned. The idea behind these agreements is to facilitate prompt and economical discovery: from the point of view of the requesting party, it reduces the delay that would be attendant to multiple levels of pre-production privilege review; from the point of view of the producing party, it reduces the costs of production by eliminating the need for many of those levels of review.

There are a number of factors, however, that limit the utility of "claw back" and "quick peek" agreements. Most important, they provide protection only in the proceeding in which they are entered. An agreement between two parties in one proceeding does not stop a third party, in a subsequent proceeding, from arguing that a waiver occurred by disclosure in the previous matter. Because the enforceability of such agreements is limited, they may do little to affect the costs of pre-production privilege review. Lawyers have to be certain that mistaken disclosures of privileged information will not result in a waiver—otherwise they have no choice but to engage in multiple levels of privilege review for all ESI.

Another limitation on such agreements is obvious—the parties must agree. Where the discoverable ESI on both sides is relatively equal, then all parties have an incentive to enter into such an agreement. But where one side has most of the data—*e.g.*, an employment discrimination case, where relevant e-mails reside on the employer's server—then the party with few (if any) documents may not be inclined to limit the costs of the adversary's pre-production privilege review. (Nonetheless, if the plaintiff-employee has an interest in *expedited* discovery, then the absence of a non-waiver agreement will result in significant delay based on the need for a full pre-production privilege review).

C. THE USE OF COURT ORDERS TO PROTECT AGAINST WAIVER BY DISCLOSURE IN DISCOVERY

Because party agreements to protect against waiver are not enforceable against non-parties, court orders are necessary to assure the parties of a clear and predictable protection against waiver. If a court can order that disclosures of privileged information do not constitute a waiver, then the parties can reduce the cost of pre-production privilege review of millions of electronic records, and can expedite the discovery process.

Rule 502(d) provides as follows:

A federal court may order that the [attorney-client privilege or work product protection] is not waived by disclosure connected with the litigation pending before the court—*in which event the disclosure is also not a waiver in any other federal or state proceeding.*

Thus, if a federal court enters an order in a litigation that disclosures by the litigants are not waivers, the parties to the proceeding receive full protection. They need not be concerned that a party in the current—or any subsequent—proceeding can use the privileged information based on a waiver. Accordingly, they can limit the costs of their pre-production privilege review.

Note that Rule 502(d) provides that the federal court's confidentiality order is controlling even in subsequent *state* proceedings. That coverage is necessary because if a state court could find that a party made a waiver in a federal proceeding—despite a federal court's protective order—then the parties could not rely on the federal order and would have to revert to costly measures to protect against mistaken disclosure of privileged information. Note also that Rule 502(d) protection is *not limited to inadvertent disclosures*. The order may provide that even intentional disclosures are not waivers—thus allowing parties to engage in "claw back" and "quick peek" arrangements.

Of course, parties can still argue that the disclosed material was never privileged in the first place. Rule 502(d) covers only the question of waiver. The privileged status of any particular document is still determined by federal common law, pursuant to the terms of Federal Rule of Evidence 501.

Under Rule 502(d), the federal court may simply enter an order that memorializes an agreement already reached by the parties—thus assuring that the agreement will bind third-parties in subsequent litigation. But the power to enter an order is not conditioned on agreement among the parties to the proceeding. The court can enter a protective order *sua sponte*, or at the request of one party and over the objection of another.

Rule 502(d) does not set forth any criteria a court must consider before entering an order protecting against waiver. The decision to enter such an order is within the discretion of the court. Any argument to the court for an order protecting against waiver should refer to at least the following factors—presumably at the Rule 16 conference where electronic discovery issues are now discussed:

- The amount of electronic information to be reviewed and produced—the greater the amount, the more necessary the protective order.

- The estimated expense for privilege review in the absence of a protective order.

- The real risk that disclosed information will be used in other proceedings—*i.e.*, how many actions or potential actions exist in which the privileged information might be relevant? If the risk is minimal, the court may find that an agreement between the parties will provide sufficient protection.

- The degree to which discovery will be accelerated by an order protecting against waiver. The less extensive the pre-production privilege review, the quicker the discovery can be expected.

A discussion with the court about an order protecting against waiver may sometimes dovetail with a discussion about cost-shifting. Often parties ask for cost-shifting at least in part because of the high cost of pre-production privilege review. The court may respond that cost-shifting on that ground is not necessary because it will enter an order under Rule 502(d).

One final point on court orders—the protection of Rule 502(d) covers only disclosures made in the proceeding in which the order is entered. There is no protection regarding subsequent disclosures of the same information—so if there is a disclosure in case 1 with an order in place, all it means is that a party in case 2 cannot argue that there was a waiver by that previous disclosure. But the party can argue that a disclosure of the same information in case 2, or in any other circumstance, constitutes a waiver. The limited protection of Rule 502(d) must especially be considered in parallel state and federal proceedings. Disclosure of the material pursuant to a court order in a federal proceeding will bind the state court—but a waiver could be found by a separate disclosure of the same information in the state court.

D. OBLIGATIONS OF THE PARTY WHO RECEIVES MISTAKENLY DISCLOSED PRIVILEGED INFORMATION

What are the obligations of a party who receives information in discovery that appears to be privileged—and there is no agreement or court order providing protection against mistaken disclosure? Rule 26(b)(5)(B) of the Federal Rules of Civil Procedure provides some guidance for parties who receive what appears to be mistakenly disclosed privileged information in these circumstances. The Rule states that if a receiving party is *notified* of the mistaken disclosure by the adversary, then the receiving party "must promptly return, sequester, or destroy the specified information and any copies it has; must not use or disclose the information until the claim [*i.e.*, whether it is privileged information at all and whether the privilege has been waived] is resolved." The receiving party may submit the materials to the court under seal to obtain a ruling as to whether the information is protected.

What happens if counsel reviews the information and *does not* think that it is privileged, and sends it to IT to be added to the spreadsheets being prepared for the litigation; or sends it to an expert who plugs the information into her calculations? Then counsel receives a call from the other side claiming privilege? In that case, Rule 26(b)(5)(B) requires the receiving party "to take reasonable steps to retrieve the information if the party disclosed it before being notified." Rule 26 does not explicitly provide for any remedy to the receiving party—but a court certainly has discretion to order some reimbursement as a condition of protecting the privileged information. Moreover, the burden on the receiving party can be taken into account in the fairness analysis of whether to find that the privilege has been waived.

If retrieving the information would be cost-prohibitive for the receiving party, a court might be justified in finding that the party who made the mistaken disclosure has waived the privilege under Rule 502(b).

Note that Rule 26 does not require the receiving party to inform the adversary that it appears to have mistakenly disclosed privileged information. But Rule 4.4(b) of the ABA Model Rules of Professional Conduct imposes an ethical obligation on the receiving party to notify the adversary of the mistake: "A lawyer who receives a document relating to the representation of the lawyer's client and knows or reasonably should know that the document was inadvertently sent shall promptly notify the sender."

CHAPTER IX

ADMISSIBILITY OF DIGITAL EVIDENCE

A. INTRODUCTION

Digital evidence is now offered in virtually every trial. Examples include e-mails, spreadsheets, evidence from web sites, digitally-enhanced photographs, powerpoint presentations, and computer-generated versions of disputed events. This Chapter addresses whether digital evidence presents admissibility problems different from those associated with traditional "hardcopy" forms of evidence. Basic familiarity with the Federal Rules of Evidence is assumed.

B. HOW IS DIGITAL EVIDENCE USED IN COURT?

Parties most commonly use digital evidence in the following ways:

• *Electronic business records:* Almost all businesses now keep their records in electronic form. Even if the records are offered in hardcopy, the underlying information is almost always generated and stored electronically.

• *Computer-generated animation illustrating how a disputed event may have occurred:* Where the litigation involves an accident or injury, a party may wish to present a computer-generated simulation of how the party maintains the event occurred, ideally based on scientific principles and reliable data.

• *Digital presentation to illustrate an expert's opinion:* Expert testimony is often technical, boring and difficult to understand. The use of digital evidence—graphics, powerpoint presentations, modeling—can help enliven and elucidate the expert's testimony for the fact finder.

• *Pedagogical device:* A digital presentation may be offered as a pedagogical device, either to summarize the trial evidence to the party's advantage, or to aid in questioning a witness. For example, a graphic may show the timing of certain telephone calls or e-mails, or a highlighted clause of a contract.

• *Digital enhancement:* Certain media, such as photos and recordings, are sometimes digitally enhanced to make them easier to read, view, or hear, or to highlight some aspect that the proponent wishes to emphasize. Digital image processing can correct blurs, sharpen details, enhance colors, enlarge features and optimize contrast. For example, a fuzzy, poorly lighted surveillance photo may be digitally enhanced to improve its visual quality.

• *Information found on the Internet:* Information on the Internet can be relevant in a litigation. For example, if a party makes a damaging statement on a web site, or in a chat room, an adversary may offer this statement. If a party wants to prove the price of a stock on a certain day, that information is available on the Internet.

• *E-mails:* It is undisputed that e-mails have substantial evidentiary value.

• *Other:* The above list is not exclusive. Other examples of the use of digital evidence include: Global Positioning System device data to locate a person or car at a particular time; a Wikipedia entry used as the basis of an expert's opinion; metadata found in Microsoft Word documents; and information found in PDAs.

C. WHICH EVIDENTIARY RULES ARE MOST OFTEN INVOKED WHEN DIGITAL EVIDENCE IS PROFFERED?

Discussion of any special concern raised by digital evidence focuses on five basic evidentiary concepts:

1. ***Relevance and Prejudice***: Digital presentations may diminish the relevance of the underlying evidence and raise a risk of unfair prejudice because these presentations may present facts in a distorted or inaccurate manner. Federal courts address such concerns under Rule 403, which provides that evidence may be excluded "if its probative value is substantially outweighed by the danger of unfair prejudice, confusion of the issues, or misleading the jury, or by considerations of undue delay, waste of time, or needless presentation of cumulative evidence."

2. *Authenticity*: To be admissible, evidence must be what the proponent says it is. Assume the government in a criminal case wants to introduce an e-mail that it claims defendant sent and that contains incriminating admissions. But if another person wrote the e-mail then the e-mail is irrelevant and inadmissible. Thus, the question of authenticity is one of conditional relevance: proffered evidence is only relevant if it is what the proponent says it is. In federal courts, most authenticity questions are addressed under Rule 901, which provides that the authenticity requirement is satisfied "by evidence sufficient to support a finding that the matter in question is what its proponent claims." Rule 901 also provides a non-exclusive list of means for establishing authenticity, such as:

- Testimony that a matter is what it is claimed to be. For example, a web site can be authenticated by a witness testifying that he visited the web site and that the printout accurately reflects what he saw.

- Appearance, contents, substance, internal patterns, or other distinctive characteristics, taken in conjunction with circumstances. For example, to prove that a party engaged in a chat room conversation, a showing that the conversation relates details that only the party could have known.

- Evidence describing a process or system used to produce a result and showing that the process or system produces an accurate result. For example, to prove the accuracy of a computer-generated distance measurement taken from a digital photograph, a showing that the computer calculated the real distance according to the correct scale.

3. *Hearsay*: Generally speaking, hearsay problems are the same for hard copy and digital records. In federal courts, hearsay issues are addressed by Rule 801 (defining hearsay, and creating exemptions for, *inter alia*, admissions by a party-opponent and certain prior statements of testifying witnesses) and by hearsay exceptions found in Rules 803, 804 and 807. Hearsay issues arise when a statement is offered to prove the truth of the matter the statement asserts. For example, assume that in an age discrimination case, plaintiff wants to introduce an e-mail from the CEO to the board of directors. The e-mail states: "We had to fire everyone over forty because they are very expensive and we need to project a younger more vibrant image." Because this is an out of court statement by the CEO, and its probative value is dependent on its truth, it is hearsay, although likely an admission of a party.

With respect to digital evidence, the most important exemption from the hearsay rule is party admissions and the most important exceptions to the hearsay rule are for business and public records. In the age-discrimination hypothetical above, the e-mail would be admissible because it is exempt from the hearsay definition under Rule 801(d)(2): it is an admission by an agent of the corporation. Similarly, a spreadsheet recording layoffs offered to prove the timing and extent of the layoffs would be admissible under the business records exception upon a showing that the record is a regular recording of a regularly conducted activity.

4. ***Best Evidence Rule***: The Best Evidence Rule states that when a party is trying to prove the *contents* of a writing, recording, or photograph, the proponent must introduce the original—unless there is an acceptable duplicate or an exception to the Rule. The Best Evidence Rule is intended to protect against fraud and manipulation. But there is no across-the-board requirement that a proponent trying to prove a point must always choose the best available evidence. A plaintiff's claim that defendant is liable for copyright infringement because defendant stole plaintiff's song provides a good example of the best evidence question. To prove the contents of his own song plaintiff must produce the original recording, which would provide the best evidence of its content. But the Best Evidence Rule has two important exceptions: (1) duplicates are acceptable unless the opponent raises a genuine question as to the original's authenticity or demonstrates that using the duplicate in lieu of the original is somehow unfair; and (2) the proponent can forego the original—or any duplicate—if there is a good reason for not having it. In federal courts, the Best Evidence Rule and its exceptions are found in Rules 1001–1004 (note that the definitions of writings and recordings covered by those rules are written to take account of digital evidence).

An example of the Best Evidence Rule as applied to digital evidence is found in *United States v. Bennett,* 363 F.3d 947 (9th Cir. 2004). The Coast Guard boarded a boat along the coast of Southern California and found drugs. At trial, the government had to prove that the boat came from Mexico in order to convict Bennett of drug importation. The government could not produce any witness who saw Bennett's boat cross the border. But Officer Chandler discovered a global positioning system ("GPS") while searching Bennett's boat and testified that the GPS revealed that Bennett's boat had traveled from Mexican waters to San Diego Bay. The GPS came with a "backtrack" feature that graphed the boat's journey that day. Chandler testified that he pressed the backtrack feature and saw the mapping of Bennett's journey from Mexican territorial waters to San Diego Bay. Chandler acknowledged, however, that he had not taken possession of the GPS device itself or obtained any record of the data contained in it. His testimony was the only evidence of the trajectory the GPS recorded.

The *Bennett* court found a violation of the Best Evidence Rule. *First*, the GPS display of the trajectory, observed by Chandler, was a writing or recording because it was a graphical representation of positional data compiled by the GPS. *Second*, Chandler did not directly observe Bennett's boat travel the path depicted by the GPS. Thus, Chandler's testimony concerned the "content" of the GPS, which, in turn, was evidence of Bennett's travels. The court concluded that "proffering testimony about Bennett's border-crossing instead of introducing the GPS data, therefore, was analogous to proffering testimony describing security camera footage of an event to prove the facts of the event instead of introducing the footage itself." To satisfy the Best Evidence Rule, the government was required to produce the GPS itself—or a printout or other representation of the GPS data. The court noted that "other evidence" of the contents of a writing or recording—such as Chandler's testimony—can substitute for the original or a duplicate if the original is shown to be lost or destroyed or otherwise unobtainable. But the government made no such showing. When asked on cross-examination to produce the GPS or its data, Chandler simply stated that he was not the GPS's custodian. He further testified that "there was no need to" videotape or photograph the data and that he had nothing other than his testimony to support his assertions about the GPS's contents. Moreover, the government presented no evidence that it would have been impossible or even difficult to download or print out the data on Bennett's GPS.

Bennett does not indicate that the Best Evidence Rule, as applied to digital evidence, is a substantial hurdle. First, the court had to find that the GPS data were being offered to prove a conclusion based directly on the data, *i.e.*, the boat's trajectory. In many cases, digital data are not offered to prove a data-dependent conclusion. For example, if the government wanted to prove that defendant had an operable system of radar detection (*e.g.*, as evidence that defendant was checking for a police presence), that testimony would not run afoul of the Best Evidence Rule because none of the data maintained in the GPS would matter. Moreover, as the court in *Bennett* notes, the Best Evidence Rule would not have been a problem if someone could have testified that he or she saw the boat come from Mexico because then the GPS data would have been cumulative or collateral. In sum, the Best Evidence Rule should only be a problem when the proponent is unprepared.

5. *Requirements for Admissible Expert Testimony*: If the probative value of digital evidence is dependent on a scientific premise or procedure, then the rule on expert testimony may apply. For example, a digital manipulation of a photo, or of forensic evidence, may require a showing that it was prepared in a scientifically reliable manner. In federal court, the basic rule on expert testimony is Rule 702, which provides that a qualified expert may testify if "(1) the testimony is based upon sufficient facts or data, (2) the testimony is the product of reliable principles and methods, and (3) the witness has applied the principles and methods reliably to the facts of the case." When presented with challenged expert evidence, the trial judge must act as a "gatekeeper" to determine whether the evidence is reliable. *See Daubert v. Merrell Dow Pharmaceuticals, Inc.*, 509 U.S. 579 (1993) (noting that trial judges should consider factors such as verifiability, peer review, rate of error, standards and controls, and general acceptance of the methods employed by an expert: "an inference or assertion must be derived by the scientific method. Proposed testimony must be supported by appropriate validation—*i.e.*, 'good grounds,' based on what is known. In short, the requirement that an expert's testimony pertain to 'scientific knowledge' establishes a standard of evidentiary reliability.").

An example of the rules on expert testimony as applied to electronic evidence is *United States v. Quinn*, 18 F.3d 1461 (9th Cir. 1994), a robbery prosecution, in which an expert used a digital process of "photogrammetry" to render an opinion about the height of the individual in surveillance photographs taken at the site of the robbery. Photogrammetry is a process in which a mathematical formula is derived by measuring the change in the dimensions of objects in a photograph as they move away from the camera. After validating the formula against objects in the photograph having known dimensions, the expert was able to make a reliable estimate of the robber's height. The court permitted the expert to testify after a proffer from the government on the basics of the photogrammetry process. Counsel for the government explained that by using vanishing points, an analyst can measure the rate of change in the size of photographic objects as they move away from a camera. After hearing the government's proffer, the court concluded that the expert used a series of computer-assisted calculations that did not involve any novel or questionable scientific techniques. The showing sufficiently met the *Daubert* test.

Even if an expert uses a reliable computer program to reach an opinion, the opinion may still be inadmissible if the expert did not employ the program properly. In *Smith v. BMW North America, Inc.*, 308 F.3d 913 (8th Cir. 2002), plaintiff alleged that her air bag malfunctioned during an accident. She proffered an accident reconstruction expert to testify that the car's velocity was great enough that the air bag should have deployed upon impact. "At the *Daubert* hearing, [the expert] testified regarding his calculations of the principal direction of force and measurements of vehicle deformation, or crush, which he entered into the EDCrash computer program to calculate the barrier equivalent velocity" of Smith's vehicle when it crashed. "The EDCrash computer program takes as input the principal direction of force, measurements of displacement in the car's structure (deformation or crush), and known data regarding the car's structure and materials from which it is manufactured. The program then outputs the barrier equivalent velocity for a given vehicle accident." The court found that the expert's opinion was properly excluded as unreliable under *Daubert* and Rule 702 because the values the expert plugged into the program were completely speculative, which meant his opinion was the product of an unreliable application of a reliable computer program.

Note that presentation of digital evidence may raise issues of reliability under *Daubert* even when it is not presented as part of an expert's testimony.

For example, if the opponent of digital evidence raises a legitimate question about the operation of a software program, the proponent may be required to show that the program produces reliable results.

D. THE GENERAL APPROACH TO DIGITAL EVIDENCE

Generally speaking, courts have not treated digital evidence any differently from any other kind of evidence. That is, the basic evidentiary principles apply: all evidence must be reliable, probative, and authentic. Most courts have rejected arguments that the digitalization of evidence has changed the playing field or rendered basic evidentiary concepts outmoded. This is so even though in its current form, the Federal Rules of Evidence generally do not explicitly treat evidence in digital form. So, for example, the learned treatise exception to the hearsay rule authorizes the court to admit "published treatises, periodicals, or pamphlets" if they are established as a reliable authority. But what if the proffered evidence is a video, DVD, or e-magazine? Despite the "paper-based" language in the learned treatise exception, federal courts have admitted evidence in electronic form under that exception if they are shown to be authoritative. The courts reason that it would be artificial to say that information sufficiently trustworthy when presented in printed form loses that badge of trustworthiness simply because it is presented in electronic form.

E. ADMISSIBILITY REQUIREMENTS FOR COMMON TYPES OF DIGITAL EVIDENCE

The following discussion describes the general treatment of the kinds of electronic evidence typically offered in the reported federal cases.

1. Business and Public Records

A business or public record is often presented in the form of a computer printout. Courts have had little problem in using Rules 803(6) (business records exception), 803(8) (public records exception) and 901/902 (rules on authenticity) to rule on the admissibility of electronic business records. Basically, an electronic business record is admissible whenever a comparable hard copy record would be admissible. They are authenticated like other records, and no special rule is required to allow the courts to rule on the admissibility or authenticity of business records. Thus, a computer printout is admissible under Rule 803(6) as a business record if the offeror establishes a sufficient foundation in the record for its introduction. *See United States v. Cestnik*, 36 F.3d 904 (10th Cir. 1994) (holding computer-generated money transfer orders admissible upon a showing by the custodian that they were regularly kept records of regularly conducted activity); *United States v. Briscoe*, 896 F.2d 1476 (7th Cir. 1990) ("It is well established that computer data compilations are admissible as business records under Fed. R.

Evid. 803(6) if a proper foundation as to the reliability of the records is established."). A party is not required to present expert testimony on the mechanical accuracy of the computer or its software; all that is necessary is to show that the computer and software is sufficiently accurate that the company relied upon it in conducting its business. *See Briscoe* (holding that regular testing of computer for internal programming errors not a prerequisite to the admission of computer records); *United States v. Moore*, 923 F.2d 910 (1st Cir. 1991) (holding that computers need not be tested for programming errors before computer records can be admitted under Rule 803(6)). *But see In re Vinhnee*, 336 B.R. 437 (B.A.P. 9th Cir. 2005) (affirming the lower court's refusal to admit computer records based on lack of authentication because plaintiff's witness "knew little about the computer software or hardware," plaintiff did not sufficiently supplement this foundational authentication defect, and the court did not "perceive testimony that [plaintiff] conducts its operations in reliance upon the accuracy of the computer in the retention and retrieval of the information in question"). Finally, electronic public records are generally admitted unless there is a substantial showing by the opponent that the records were prepared in an untrustworthy manner.

2. Machine-Generated Evidence

Information that is generated by a machine (such as a printout of the chemical breakdown of a substance, or an automatic response to an e-mail) may

be offered as proof of an event. As to the hearsay
rule: if evidence is completely machine-generated, it
is not hearsay at all, because it is not a statement
from a declarant. For example, in *United States v.
Washington*, 498 F.3d 225 (4th Cir. 2007), defendant was convicted of operating a motor vehicle
under the influence of drugs and alcohol. At trial,
an expert interpreted a printout of a gas chromatogram of defendant's blood sample, and concluded
that defendant's blood sample contained PCP and
alcohol. Defendant argued that the testimony was
hearsay because the expert had no personal knowledge of whether defendant's blood contained PCP
or alcohol—the expert just read the chromatogram.
Defendant contended that the government was required to produce the lab personnel who conducted
the test. The court rejected this argument, finding
that the printout was not hearsay because the
printout was not a statement of a witness, but
rather a statement of the chromatography machine
itself—and it would be silly to hold that the machine must be subject to cross-examination. The
court noted that the government would still have to
prove that the printout was *authentic* (*i.e.*, that the
test was actually done on defendant's blood sample), and that technicians might need to provide a
chain of custody of the samples (to counter any
argument that defendant's sample had been
switched or altered); but the court observed that
defendant made no objection to the authenticity of
the machine's report. Of course, this evidence, like

any other, must be relevant and not unduly prejudicial under Rule 403.

3. Digital Demonstrative Evidence

A computer-generated presentation (such as an animation) may be offered as proof of how an event occurred—the most prevalent example being an accident reconstruction, in which data known about the accident are entered into a computer, and a program uses the data to show what happened as to the issues in dispute. For this purpose, the use of a computer to recreate an event is no different in kind from videotaping a reconstruction of an accident or a product failure. Courts consistently apply Rule 403 to determine whether the reconstruction is based on conditions and data that are substantially similar to the original conditions—*e.g.*, if the accident occurred on a wet road, data to that effect must be entered. If the conditions are not substantially similar, the purported reconstruction, computer-generated or not, is excluded as substantially more prejudicial than probative. There might also be reliability problems due to the probable use of retained experts in creating the reconstructions. But these problems are dealt with under standard evidentiary principles.

An example of the application of Rule 403 to digital demonstrative evidence arose in *Bowoto v. Chevron Corp.*, 2006 WL 1627004 (N.D. Cal. June 12, 2006). Plaintiffs offered a three-dimensional computer model of a barge that was the location of the disputed incident. The model purported to demonstrate what the barge looked like at the time of the disputed event, and also allowed the viewer to navigate to a specific spot on the barge to see the perspective of a person standing at that viewpoint (thus to evaluate the vantage points of trial witnesses). The model was created with a program called LightWave 3D. The court found that the digital evidence was inadmissible under Rule 403 because it did not accurately represent the conditions at the time of the incident. The court noted that aerial photographs taken around the time of the incident indicated that the barge was cluttered with large objects, while the computer model presented the barge with an entirely clean deck. The court found that because of the model's inaccurate representation of the barge's deck, the use of the model to show a witness's viewpoint should be excluded under Rule 403. As an initial matter, the probative value of the model was substantially diminished by its inaccurate depiction of the barge. While the model allowed the jury to understand where a witness was and what perspective he had on the events that transpired, the jury's understanding would have been incomplete. And this incomplete understanding was likely to affirmatively mislead the jury as to what the witness could see.

The court concluded that "the computer model is a powerful tool, and, through its ability to place the jurors on the deck of the barge, runs a risk of making a strong impression on the mind of the jury." Therefore it was important to have the computer model be "as accurate as possible."

While the *Bowoto* court excluded the digital presentation, it must be remembered that Rule 403 is a rule that is geared toward *admitting* evidence: under Rule 403, relevant evidence must be admitted unless its probative value is *substantially outweighed* by the risks of prejudice, jury confusion, and delay. This means that a digital presentation need not track the underlying facts with absolute exactitude.

The South Carolina Supreme Court has articulated a sound four-part test for the admission of computer-generated animations: "We hold that a computer-generated video animation is admissible as demonstrative evidence when the proponent shows that the animation is (1) authentic under Rule 901 ...; (2) relevant under Rules 401 and 402 ...; (3) a fair and accurate representation of the evidence to which it relates, and (4) its probative value [is not] substantially [outweighed by] the danger of unfair prejudice, confusing the issues or misleading the jury under Rule 403." *Clark v. Cantrell*, 529 S.E.2d 528 (S.C. 2000) (citing Gregory P. Joseph, *A Simplified Approach to Computer–Generated Evidence and Animations*, 156 F.R.D. 327 (1994)).

4. Digital Presentation to Illustrate an Expert's Opinion or a Party's Theory of the Case

A computer-generated presentation may be offered to illustrate an expert's opinion or a party's version of the facts. For example, if an expert testifies to how a chemical substance interacts with the human body, a digital presentation that illustrates the effect may be useful to the presentation. As with any other such illustration, a computer-generated presentation may be considered by the factfinder if it helps to illustrate the expert's opinion, or a party's version of the facts, and does not purport to be a recreation of the disputed event. Again, standard evidentiary principles such as those found in Rules 403 and 702 have worked well. The jury is instructed in such cases that the computer-generated presentation is not to be considered as proof of how the event occurred, but only as an explanation of the expert's testimony or the party's theory of the case. An example of such a limiting instruction, is found in *Hinkle v. City of Clarksburg*, 81 F.3d 416 (4th Cir. 1996), a civil rights action in which plaintiffs argued that Officer Lake shot Wilson without provocation. A Forensic Animation Technologist testified for defendants to a version of the shooting that was based on his interpretation of the evidence and was consistent with the police officers' testimony. To illustrate the expert's testimony, defendants introduced a computer-animated videotape. The videotape depicted Wilson's apartment complex, the officers' position in relation to the open door to Wilson's apartment, and a step-by-step account of the incident. It showed an animated version of Officer Lake on the stairwell outside the apartment aiming his gun toward Wilson, who was moving toward the open door. It depicted Wilson raising his shotgun toward the doorway, Officer Lake firing the fatal shot, Wilson's body spinning around from the force of the shot, and his shotgun discharging into the stuffed chair in the back of the room. It then showed how the officers' version of the event was consistent with the physical evidence by concluding with a depiction of the trajectory of Officer Lake's bullet in line with the wounds to Wilson's forearm, chest, back, and the bullet hole in the wall of the room. The computer animation was not offered to prove how the event occurred. It was offered only to illustrate the expert's testimony. The jury was instructed as follows:

"This animation is not meant to be a recreation of the events, but rather it consists of a computer picture to help you understand Mr. Jason's opinion which he will, I understand, be giving later in the trial. And to reenforce the point, the video is not meant to be an exact recreation of what happened during the shooting, but rather it represents Mr. Jason's evaluation of the evidence presented." The appellate court found that the computer animation was properly admitted for this limited purpose under Rule 403.

Although there is often a fine line between a recreation of an event and an illustration of an expert's opinion, the practical distinction is the difference between a jury believing that it is seeing a repeat of the actual event and a jury understanding that it is seeing an illustration of an expert's opinion of what happened. If the digital evidence is a purported recreation, then the requirements of similarity and reliability are obviously more stringent.

5.   Pedagogical Devices

A computer-generated presentation may be offered to illustrate or summarize the trial evidence to the party's advantage, or to aid in the questioning of a witness. For example, a party might prepare a powerpoint presentation with a time line of established events, or a breakdown of a contract or transaction. Such presentations are not evidence at all, but are instead pedagogical devices. They are no different in kind from a hardcopy summary of evidence, or the low-tech pinpointing of trial testimony or critical language from documents at issue in the case. The question is whether the presentation fairly characterizes the evidence. If the presentation is unfair, computer-generated or not, it will be prohibited under Rules 403 and 611, both of which authorize the trial court to exercise discretion in regulating the presentation of evidence at trial. Because the digital presentation in these circumstances is an extension of the attorney's argument, it is subject to the same guidelines that govern what an attorney may say. Proper argument is supposed to be confined to facts introduced in evidence, facts of common knowledge, and logical inferences based on the evidence. An attorney cannot argue about facts not in the record or misstate testimony.

Local rules usually require the lawyer to disclose a pedagogical device to opposing counsel and the judge before it is presented to the jury—and at that point its basis in the evidence can be verified and if necessary the data and programming can be adjusted.

6. Summary of Voluminous Evidence

A computer-generated presentation might be offered as a summary of otherwise admissible evidence that is too voluminous to be conveniently examined in court. Such a presentation is evaluated under Rule 1006. Computer-generated summaries are treated no differently from non-computer-generated summaries for purposes of Rule 1006.

7. Digital Enhancements

Photos, videos and other "original" documents are sometimes digitally enhanced to make them easier to read, view, or hear, or to highlight some aspect that the proponent wishes to emphasize. Courts have held that the admissibility of such enhancements is governed by Rules 403, 702, 901 and 1002, with the basic question being whether the enhancement is a fair and accurate depiction of the original. For example, in *United States v. Sei-*

fert, 445 F.3d 1043 (8th Cir. 2006), an arson prosecution, the court held that a digitally-enhanced
surveillance tape was admissible to prove that defendant committed the crime. The surveillance
tape was found in the rubble of the fire; the retrieved video picture was dark and the perpetrator
was hard to make out. After the tape was digitally
brightened, defendant became clearly visible. At a
hearing on admissibility, the government presented
the agent who conducted the digital enhancement.
He was an expert in electronic surveillance and
video analysis. He described the computer program
that enhanced the image. Because the original video was "time lapsed"—slower than normal speed—
the expert "real-timed" the enhanced copy. He
also explained that the original video was a "quad
image," with the screen divided into quarters to
depict images from four cameras. The expert en-
larged the video from the relevant camera, discard-
ing the output from the three irrelevant ones. Finally, because the original image was dark, the
expert brightened it, additionally brightening the
suspect and the surrounding area more than the
rest of the image. On cross-examination, the expert
maintained that he simply enhanced the original
video and did not manipulate it. The court noted
that while the technician brightened the video, he
did not brighten *only* defendant but also the surrounding area, thus preserving their "relative
brightness." It held that there was no showing
that the enhancement rendered the video "inau-
thentic or untrustworthy." Similarly, in *United*

States v. Beeler, 62 F. Supp. 2d 136 (D. Me. 1999), the court admitted digitally-enhanced videotapes over a best evidence objection, where the enhancements omitted extraneous frames and made the images larger, clearer, and easier to view. The court noted that "the edited and enhanced versions of the Mobil Mini–Mart surveillance videotape are admissible because they have been proven accurate and serve to present the substance of the original videotape in a more easily understood form, which is in accord with the spirit of the best evidence rule."

8. Internet Evidence[1]

There are three forms of Internet data typically offered into evidence—(1) data posted on the web site by the owner of the site ("web site data"); (2) data posted by others with the owner's consent (*e.g.*, a chat room); and (3) data posted by others without the owner's consent ("hacker" material). The wrinkle for authenticity purposes is that, because Internet data are electronic, they can be manipulated and offered into evidence in distorted forms. Additionally, various hearsay concerns are implicated, depending on the purpose for which the proffer is made.

1. The following discussion on Internet evidence (and also the later discussion on e-mail evidence) is adapted from Gregory Joseph, Esq.'s article, *Internet and E-mail Evidence*. We are grateful to Mr. Joseph for allowing us use of this material. Further developments can be found on Mr. Joseph's blog, *available at* http://www.josephnyc.com.

a. Authentication of Internet Evidence

i. Web Site Data. Information posted on web sites is often relevant to matters in litigation—for example, a government web site may publish data about economic conditions. Web site evidence must be authenticated in all cases, and, depending on the use for which the offer is made, hearsay concerns may be implicated.

The authentication standard is no different for web site data or chat room evidence than for any other type of data. Under Rule 901(a), "The requirement of authentication ... is satisfied by evidence sufficient to support a finding that the matter in question is what its proponent claims."

In applying this rule to web site evidence, there are three questions that must be answered, explicitly or implicitly:

1.   What was actually on the web site?

2.   Does the exhibit or testimony accurately reflect what was on the web site?

3.   If so, is the exhibit or testimony attributable to the owner of the site?

In the first instance, authenticity can be established by the testimony of any witness that the witness typed in the URL associated with the website; that he or she logged on to the site and reviewed what was there; and that a printout or other exhibit fairly and accurately reflects what the witness saw. This last testimony is no different than that required to authenticate a photograph, other replica or demonstrative exhibit. The witness may be lying or mistaken, but that is true of all testimony and a principal reason for cross-examination. Unless the opponent of the evidence raises a genuine issue as to trustworthiness, testimony of this sort is sufficient to satisfy Rule 901(a), presumptively authenticating the web site data and shifting the burden of refuting the evidence to the opponent. It is reasonable to presume that material on a web site (other than chat room conversations) was placed there by the owner of the site.

The opponent of the evidence must, in fairness, be free to challenge that presumption by raising facts showing that the proffered evidence does not accurately reflect the contents of a web site, or that those contents are not attributable to the owner of the site. *First*, even if the proffer fairly reflects what was on the site, the data proffered may have been manipulated by hackers. *Second*, the proffer may not fairly reflect what was on the site due to modification in the proffered exhibit or testimony.

Detecting modifications of electronic evidence can be very difficult. That does not mean, however, that nothing is admissible because everything is subject to distortion. The possibility of alteration is raised with many kinds of evidence, from testimony to photographs to digital images, but that does not render everything inadmissible. It merely accentuates the need for judges to focus on all relevant circumstances in assessing admissibility, and to leave random concerns about alterations to the jury.

In considering whether the opponent has raised a genuine issue as to authenticity, and whether the proponent has satisfied it, the court will look at the totality of the circumstances, including, for example:

- The length of time the data were posted on the site.

- Whether others report having seen them.

- Whether they remain on the web site for the court to verify.

- Whether the data are of a type ordinarily posted on that web site or web sites of similar entities (*e.g.*, financial information from corporations).

- Whether the owner of the site has elsewhere published the same data, in whole or in part.

- Whether others have published the same data, in whole or in part.

- Whether the data have been republished by others who identify the source of the data as the web site in question.

A genuine question as to authenticity may be established circumstantially. For example, more authentication may be reasonably required from a proponent of Internet evidence who is a skilled computer user and who is suspected of having modified the proffered web site data for purposes of creating false evidence.

In assessing the authenticity of web site data, important evidence is normally available from the personnel managing the web site ("webmaster" personnel). A webmaster can establish that a particular file was placed on the web site at a specific time through direct testimony or through documentation, which may be generated automatically by the software of the web server. It is possible that the content provider—the author of the material appearing on the site—will be someone other than the person who loaded the file. In that event, this second witness (or set of documentation) may be necessary to reasonably ensure that the content that appeared on the site is the same as that proffered.

ii.   Self-Authentication.   Government offices publish an abundance of reports, press releases and other information on their official web sites. Internet publication of a governmental document on an official web site constitutes an "official publication" covered by Rule 902(5). Under that Rule, official publications of government offices are self-authenticating—no further evidence other than the document itself is necessary to establish authenticity.

iii.   Chat Room Evidence.   A proffer of chat room postings generally implicates the same authenticity issues discussed above in connection with web site data, but with a twist. While it is reasonable to presume that the contents of a web site are attributable to the site's owner, the same cannot be said for chat room evidence. By definition, chat room postings are not made by the owner of the site. Further, chat room participants usually use screen names (pseudonyms) rather than their real names.

Chat room evidence is often used at trial to prove what the chatter said—there are a number of cases, for example, in which criminal defendants are alleged to have traded child pornography in a chat room conversation. The evidentiary question in such cases is whether the government can show that defendant made the incriminating statements. This is a question of authenticity, *i.e.*, that the chat room statement is what the government says it is, a statement by defendant. Evidence sufficient to support a finding that a particular individual made a chat room posting may include, for example:

• Evidence that the individual used the screen name in question when participating in chat room conversations (either generally or at the site in question).

• Evidence that, when a meeting with the person using the screen name was arranged, the individual in question showed up.

• Evidence that the person using the screen name identified herself as the individual (in chat room conversations or otherwise), especially if that identification is coupled with particularized information unique to the individual, such as a street address or e-mail address.

• Evidence that the individual had in his possession information given to the person using the screen name (such as contact information provided by the police in a sting operation).

• Evidence from the hard drive of the individual's computer reflecting that a user of the computer used the screen name in question.

With respect to the dialog itself, a participant in the chat room conversation may authenticate a transcript with testimony based on firsthand knowledge that the transcript fairly and accurately captures the chat. *See Ford v. State*, 617 S.E.2d 262 (Ga. Ct. App. 2005), where the court explained:

We find this situation analogous to the admission of a videotape, which is admissible where the operator of the machine which produced it, or one who personally witnessed the events recorded, testifies that the videotape accurately portrayed what the witness saw take place at the time the events occurred. Here, [the witness] personally witnessed the real-time chat recorded in Transcript B as it was taking place, and he testified that the transcript accurately represented the on-line conversation. Under these circumstances, [his] testimony was tantamount to that of a witness to an event and was sufficient to authenticate the transcript.

iv. Internet Archives. Web sites change over time. Lawsuits focus on particular points in time. The relevant web page may be changed or deleted before litigation begins. Various Internet archive services exist that provide snapshots of web pages at various points in time. To the extent that those services, in the ordinary course of their business, accurately retrieve and store copies of the web site as it appeared at specified points in time, the stored web pages are admissible. The certification should contain the same elements as set forth above on authenticating web site data, with necessary modifications (*e.g.*, the retrieval process may be automated, requiring authentication of the automated function, such as proving that it is used and relied on in the ordinary course of business and produces reliable results).

v. Temporary Internet Files. When a computer user accesses the Internet, web browsers like Microsoft Internet Explorer temporarily store all accessed images in a "temporary" folder so that, if the computer user attempts to view the same web page again, the computer is able to retrieve the page more quickly. Even deleted images in the temporary folder may be retrieved and viewed by an expert using an appropriate program, and expert testimony about this process is sufficient to authenticate the images.

vi. Search Engines. The results generated by widely recognized search engines, like Google or Yahoo!, may be pertinent in litigation—*e.g.*, a trademark action to show dilution of a mark or a privacy/right of publicity action to show appropriation of a likeness. Proper authentication consists of testimony or a certification from a witness that the witness typed the web site address of the search engine; that he or she logged on to the site; the precise search run by the witness; that the witness reviewed the results of the search; and that a printout or other exhibit fairly and accurately reflects those results. The witness should be someone capable of further averring that she, or the witness's employer, uses the search engine in the ordinary course of business and that it produces accurate results. Further, the testimony or certification should reflect that the witness logged onto some of the web sites identified by the search engine to demonstrate, as a circumstantial matter, that the particular search generated accurate results.

b. Hearsay Issues with Respect to Internet Evidence

Authenticity aside, every extrajudicial statement drawn from a web site has been made out of court, and so must satisfy a hearsay exception or exemption if offered for the truth of the matter it asserts. *See United States v. Jackson*, 208 F.3d 633 (7th Cir. 2000) ("The web postings were not statements made by declarants testifying at trial, and they were being offered to prove the truth of the matter asserted. That means they were hearsay."); *Monotype Imaging, Inc. v. Bitstream, Inc.*, 376 F. Supp. 2d 877, 884–85 (N.D. Ill. 2005) ("The Court refused to admit Exhibits 15 and 17 for the truth of the matter asserted in them because these exhibits are inadmissible hearsay. The Court admitted Exhibits 15 and 17 only for the limited purpose of proving that the diagrams in those exhibits were displayed on the respective web sites on the dates indicated on the exhibits.").

Note that there is no hearsay problem in establishing that material *appeared* on a web site; it is sufficient for a witness with knowledge to testify that the witness logged onto the site and to describe what he or she saw. But if the assertions on the web site are offered to prove their underlying truth, then the hearsay rule must be satisfied.

i. Data Entry. Some web site data are entered into Internet-readable format in the same way that a bookkeeper may enter numbers into a computer. This act of data entry is an extrajudicial statement—*i.e.*, assertive non-verbal conduct—which means that the product is hearsay when offered for the truth of the matter asserted. Each level of hearsay must satisfy the hearsay rule, so the act of data entry must be addressed separately from the content of the posted declaration.

Data entry is usually a regularly-conducted activity within Rule 803(6) (or, in the context of a government office, it falls within Rule 803(8) (public records exception)). The real question about the data entry function is its accuracy. This is, in substance, an issue of authenticity and should be addressed as part of the requisite authentication foundation whenever a genuine doubt as to trustworthiness has been raised. If the foundational evidence establishes that the data have been entered accurately, the hearsay objection to the data entry function should ordinarily be overruled.

When a webmaster simply transfers an image or digitally converts an electronic file into web format, this is a technical process that does not involve an assertion within the definition of hearsay and is best judged as purely an authentication issue. The difference, analytically, is between the grocery store clerk who punches the price into the check-out computer (this is assertive non-verbal conduct), and the clerk who simply scans the price into the computer (non-assertive behavior). Only assertive non-verbal conduct raises hearsay issues and requires an applicable hearsay exception or exemption.

ii.   Business and Public Records on a Web Site.   Businesses and government offices publish countless documents on their web sites in the ordinary course of business. Provided that all of the traditional criteria are met, these documents will satisfy the hearsay exception for "records" of the business or public office involved, under Rules 803(6) or (8). Reliability and trustworthiness are said to be presumptively established by the fact of actual reliance in the regular course of an enterprise's activities. As long as the web site data constitute business or public records, this quality is not lost simply because the printout or other image that is proffered into evidence was generated for litigation purposes. Each digital data entry contained on the web site is itself a Rule 803(6) or (8) "record" because it is a "data compilation, in any form." Consequently, if each entry has been made in conformance with Rules 803(6) or (8), the proffered output satisfies the hearsay exception even if it: (a) was not printed out at or near the time of the events recorded (as long as the entries were timely made), (b) was not prepared in ordinary course (but, *e.g.*, for trial), and (c) is not in the usual form (but, *e.g.*, has been converted into graphic form). When data are simply produced in a printout, they do not lose their business-record character. To the extent that significant selection, correction and interpretation are involved, their reliability and authenticity may be questioned.

iii. Market Reports and Tables. Rule 803(17) provides a hearsay exception for "market quotations, tabulations, lists, directories, or other published compilations, generally used and relied upon by the public or by persons in particular occupations." A number of cases have applied this Rule to commercial web sites furnishing such data as interest rates and Blue Book prices of used cars. This rationale plainly extends to the other sorts of traditional information admitted under Rule 803(17), such as tables reflecting the prices of items like stocks, bonds and currency; real estate listings; and telephone books.

iv. Admissions. Web site data published by a litigant comprise admissions of that litigant when offered by an opponent, thus within the hearsay exemption for admissions by a party-opponent. Accordingly, even if the owner of a web site may not offer data from the site into evidence, because the proffer is hearsay when the owner attempts to do so (unless offered to rebut a charge of fabrication, improper influence, or motive under 801(d)(1)(B)), an opposing party is authorized to offer it as an admission of the owner under 801(d)(2)(A).

v.   Non-Hearsay Proffers.   Not uncommonly, web site data is offered not for the truth of the matter asserted but merely to show that the data were published on the web, either by one of the litigants or by unaffiliated non-parties. For example, in a punitive damages proceeding, the fact of Internet publication may be relevant to show that defendant published defamatory statements for the public to rely on. Or, in a trademark action, Internet listings or advertisements may be relevant on the issue of consumer confusion or purchaser understanding. In neither of these circumstances is the web site data offered for its truth. Accordingly, no hearsay issues arise.

9.   E-mail Evidence

E-mails are obviously important in many litigations. For example, in the prosecution of Arthur Andersen for obstruction of justice arising out of the Enron debacle, the critical piece of evidence was an e-mail from a lawyer suggesting the need for document destruction. And in suits alleging sex discrimination, e-mails sent by supervisors are often offered to show discriminatory intent.

Like Internet evidence, e-mails raise both authentication and hearsay issues. The general principles of admissibility are essentially the same, because e-mail is simply a distinctive type of Internet evidence—namely, the use of the Internet to send personalized communications.

a. Authentication of E-mail

The authenticity of e-mails is governed by Rule 901(a), which requires only "evidence sufficient to support a finding that the matter in question is what its proponent claims." As discussed above, the threshold for establishing authenticity is not high. For example, in *United States v. Safavian,* 435 F. Supp. 2d 36 (D.D.C. 2006), the court analyzed the admissibility of e-mail, noting as follows:

> The question for the court under Rule 901 is whether the proponent of the evidence has "offered a foundation from which the jury could reasonably find that the evidence is what the proponent says it is." ... The Court need not find that the evidence is necessarily what the proponent claims, but only that there is sufficient evidence that the *jury* ultimately might do so.

Note that under Rule 901(b)(4), e-mail may be authenticated by reference to its "appearance, contents, substance, internal patterns, or other distinctive characteristics, taken in conjunction with circumstances." *See United States v. Siddiqui,* 235 F.3d 1318 (11th Cir. 2000) (allowing the authentication of an e-mail by circumstantial evidence, including: the presence of defendant's work e-mail address; content in the e-mail that defendant was familiar with; use of defendant's nickname in the e-mail; and testimony by witnesses that defendant spoke to them about the subjects contained in the e-mail).

If e-mail is produced by a party from the party's files and on its face purports to have been sent by that party, these circumstances alone are ordinarily sufficient to establish authenticity—so, for example, if an e-mail is produced by a party in discovery, that production is enough to indicate that the e-mail is what the producer says it is. Authenticity may also be established by testimony of a witness who sent or received the e-mails—in essence, that the e-mails are the personal correspondence of the witness.

It is important, for authentication purposes, that e-mail generated by a business or other entity facially reflects the identity of the organization. The name of the organization, usually in some abbreviated form, ordinarily appears in the e-mail address of the sender (after the @ symbol). This mark of origin has been held to authenticate the e-mail as having been sent by the organization, under Rule 902(7), which provides that the following is sufficiently authenticated: "Inscriptions, signs, tags, or labels purporting to have been affixed in the course of business and indicating ownership, control, or origin." Where the e-mail reflects the entire e-mail name of a party (and not just the mark of origin), it has been held to comprise a party admission of origin.

Independently, circumstantial indicia that may suffice to establish that proffered e-mails were sent, or were sent by a specific person, include evidence that:

- A witness or entity received the e-mail.

- The e-mail bore the customary format of an e-mail, including the addresses of the sender and recipient.

- The address of the recipient is consistent with the e-mail address on other e-mails sent by the same sender.

- The e-mail contained the typewritten name or nickname of the recipient (and, perhaps, the sender) in the body of the e-mail or as an electronic signature.

- The e-mail recited matters that would normally be known only to the individual who is alleged to have sent it (or to a discrete number of persons including this individual).

- Following receipt of the e-mail, the recipient witness had a discussion with the individual who purportedly sent it, and the conversation reflected this individual's knowledge of the contents of the e-mail.

Transcriptions of e-mail or text message exchanges, the originals of which have been lost through no fault of the proponent, may be authenticated by testimony of a witness with knowledge that he or she transcribed them and that they accurately reflect the contents of the e-mail or text message exchange.

There are a variety of technical means by which e-mail transmissions may be traced. Therefore, if serious authentication issues arise, a technical witness may be of assistance. This may become important, for example, in circumstances where a person or entity denies sending an e-mail, or denies receipt of an e-mail and has not engaged in conduct that furnishes circumstantial evidence of receipt (such as a subsequent communication reflecting knowledge of the contents of the e-mail).

While it is true that an e-mail may be sent by anyone who, with a password, gains access to another's e-mail account, similar uncertainties exist with virtually all documents and do not preclude admissibility. *See, e.g.*, *Interest of F.P.*, 878 A.2d 91 (Pa. Super. Ct. 2005) (just as an e-mail can be faked, a "signature can be forged; a letter can be typed on another's typewriter; distinct letterhead stationery can be copied or stolen. We believe that e-mail messages and similar forms of electronic communication can be properly authenticated within the existing framework [of Rule 901].").

b. Hearsay Issues Concerning E-mail

The hearsay issues associated with e-mail are largely the same as those associated with conventional correspondence. An e-mail offered for the truth of the matter asserted is hearsay and must satisfy an applicable hearsay exemption or exception. The prevalence and ease of use of e-mail, particularly in the business setting, makes it attractive simply to assume that all e-mail generated at or by a business falls under the business records exception to the hearsay rule. That assumption is incorrect. For example, in *United States v. Ferber*, 966 F. Supp. 90 (D. Mass. 1997), the government offered into evidence a multi-paragraph e-mail from a subordinate to his superior describing a telephone conversation with defendant (not a fellow employee). In that conversation, defendant inculpated himself, and the e-mail so reflected. The court rejected the proffer under the business records exception because, "while it may have been [the employee's] routine business practice to make such records, there was no sufficient evidence that [his employer] required such records to be maintained.... [I]n order for a document to be admitted as a business record, there must be some evidence of a business duty to make and regularly maintain records of this type." *See also Monotype Corp. v. International Typeface Corp.*, 43 F.3d 443 (9th Cir. 1994) ("E-mail is far less of a systematic business activity than a monthly inventory printout.").

*i. **Hearsay Within Hearsay.*** Because e-mails are written without regard for the rules of evidence, they commonly contain multiple layers of hearsay. Under Rule 805, each layer of hearsay must independently satisfy an exception to the hearsay rule. Absent that, any hearsay portion of an e-mail that is offered for its truth will be excluded. Consider *State of New York v. Microsoft Corp.*, 2002

WL 650047 (D.D.C. Apr. 12, 2002), where the court explained:

> "If both the source and the recorder of the information, as well as every other participant in the chain producing the record, are acting in the regular course of business, the multiple hearsay is excused by Rule 803(6). If the source of the information is an outsider, Rule 803(6) does not, by itself, permit the admission of the business record. The outsider's statement must fall within another hearsay exception to be admissible because it does not have the presumption of accuracy that statements made during the regular course of business have."

ii. Admission of Party Opponent. Under Rule 801(d)(2), e-mails sent by party opponents constitute admissions and are not excluded by the hearsay rule. The e-mail address itself, which reflects that it originates from a party, may be admissible as a party admission. Further, an e-mail from a party opponent that forwards another e-mail may comprise an adoptive admission of the original message, depending on the text of the forwarding e-mail. *See Sea–Land Services, Inc. v. Lozen International, LLC*, 285 F.3d 808 (9th Cir. 2002) (one of plaintiff's employees "incorporated and adopted the contents" of an e-mail message from another of plaintiff's employees when she forwarded it to defendant with a cover note that "manifested an adoption or belief in [the] truth" of the information contained in the original e-mail, within Rule 801(d)(2)(B)). If there is not an adoptive admission, however, the forwarded e-mail chain may comprise hearsay-within-hearsay.

iii. Non-Hearsay Uses. Not all extrajudicial statements are hearsay. The contents of an authenticated e-mail may, for example, constitute a verbal act—*e.g.*, defamation or the offer or acceptance of a contract—in which case the statement is not offered for its truth but rather for the fact it was made. Also an e-mail may itself reflect the conduct at issue and accordingly is a verbal act and not hearsay. *See United States v. Safavian*, 435 F. Supp. 2d 36 (D.D.C. 2006) (certain e-mails themselves comprised "lobbying work" of defendant Jack Abramoff).

E-mail may be admitted for the non-hearsay purpose of proving the effect on a reader. For example, assume that Joe sues Officer Bill for arresting him without probable cause. Officer Bill offers an e-mail he received from Joe's cousin, stating "I saw Joe kill his wife." That e-mail can be offered not to show that Joe actually killed his wife, but rather for the fact that Officer Bill used the information as a basis for arresting Joe.

———

For more on admissibility issues attendant to digital evidence, see *Lorraine v. Markel American Insurance Co.*, 241 F.R.D. 534 (D. Md. 2007), in which the court provides a thorough and detailed analysis of all the evidence rules that bear on the admissibility of digital evidence.

*

INDEX

331

AUTHENTICATION—Cont'd
Forensic authentication, 27, 60, 158, 164
Metadata as authenticity tool, 60, 158, 164
Producer authentication of e-mail, 324

AUTOMATED RECORDS MANAGEMENT SYSTEM (ARMS)
Generally, 4

AUTOMATICALLY CREATED ESI
Definition, 7
Storage methods, 6

BACKUP SYSTEMS
Archiving and
        Generally, 20
    See also Archival Data, this index
Continuous backups, 25
Differential backups, 24
Enterprise backups, 22
Full backups, 23
Good cause for discovery, 20
Guidelines for electronic discovery, 114
Incremental backups, 23
Internet backup, 22
Investigations of, 127
Local backups, 22
Real-time backups, 25
Reasonable accessibility standards, 20
Record Retention Policies, this index
Rotation backups, 25
Strategies, 20
Structured and unstructured, 21
Tapes
    Accessibility, 185
    Accessibility determinations, 196
    Data-downgrading, 201
    Disaster recovery systems, accessibility determinations, 196
    Duplicate information and duty to preserve, 38
    Marginal utility test of reasonable accessibility, 192
    Possession, custody, or control determinations, 92
    Preservation costs and reasonably accessible ESI determina-
        tions, 57
    Reasonably accessible ESI, 53
    Restoration costs, 199
    Rotation schema, 26
Types of schemas, 23

COSTS—Cont'd
Preservation costs affecting accessibility, 57
Privilege reviews, pre-production, 275
Restoration costs, determining, 57
Restoration of backups, 199
Sanction awards of costs, 216, 238
Seven factor cost-shifting test, 196
Sharing and shifting, 194
2006 Amendments, 196
Undue burden or expense determinations, 196
Voluminous production, search costs, 3

COURT ORDERS
Confidentiality orders, 282
Inadvertent waiver protections, 281
On-site inspections orders, 170
Overbroad production, orders directing Bates numbering, 136
Preservation Orders, this index
Privileged data procedures, inclusion in, 104
Sanctions, this index
Scheduling orders, 106

CROSS-BORDER PRODUCTION
 Generally, 207
Aerospatiale factors, 212
Blocking statutes, 208
EU Data Protection Directive, 208
FRCP/Hague Convention conflicts, 209
Privacy laws applicable, 207

CUSTODIAN-BASED APPLICATIONS
Messaging system ESI, 8

CUSTODIAN-BASED ESI
Definition, 7
Storage methods, 7

CUSTODIAN-CENTRIC DATA STORAGE
Definition, 17
Storage methods, 17

CUSTODY
See Possession, Custody, or Control, this index

CUSTOMER RELATIONSHIP MANAGEMENT (CRM) SOFT-WARE
Enterprise applications, 11

†